FROM THE MOUNTAINS TO THE PLAINS

The Integration of the Lafofa Nuba
into Sudanese Society

Leif O. Manger

Nordiska Afrikainstitutet, Uppsala 1994
(The Scandinavian Institute of African Studies)

Indexing terms
Anthropology
Ethnic groups
Nuba [people]
Traditional culture
Agricultural system
Adaptation to change
Cultural integration
Social integration
Sudan
Liri region, Sudan

Cover: Adriaan Honcoop
Language editing: Madi Gray
Copyediting: Sonja Johansson

Printed in Sweden by
Motala Grafiska AB, Motala, 1994

ISBN 91-7106-336-6

Contents

LIST OF MAPS

LIST OF FIGURES

LIST OF TABLES

Preface

This book fills a gap in the ethnography of the Nuba Mountains of the Sudan. It presents the first comprehensive ethnographic record of a matrilineal Nuba group, the Lafofa. It also contains the first presentation of the Liri region in which the Lafofa live. Being in the very south of the Nuba Mountain area, Liri is to the south of the areas visited by Sigfried Nadel and described in his classic monograph on the Nuba (Nadel, 1947). Liri also lies beyond the areas that have received attention in more recent anthropological works, such as that by Gerd Baumann in Miri (1987), Jim Faris in Kao-Nyaro (1989), Mohamed Salih (1983) and Richard Rottenburg (1988) among the the Moro groups. Thus the study to be presented here adds to our knowledge of the Nuba Mountains area and hopefully further adds to our understanding of this culturally complex region.

The major part of the fieldwork for the study was undertaken in 1979 and 1980, and supplemented by shorter field visits up until 1984. The situation in the Nuba Mountains and in Liri at that time differed dramatically from how it is today, with the Nuba Mountains being a battlefield in the Sudanese Civil War. During my last visit to the Lafofa in 1984, a newly established Sudan Government military camp bore witness to the fact that the Liri area was becoming involved in the escalating war between the Sudanese government and the Southern Peoples Liberation Army (SPLA). The war had been going on in the Southern Sudan since 1983 and the SPLA wanted to spread the resistance to areas within the North. The southern parts of the Nuba Mountains were among the first areas to experience this. In the years after 1984 the Nuba Mountains area increasingly became a battlefield of this tragic civil war.

As in all wars the civilian population is suffering. Reports from human rights organizations indicate that atrocities are taking place, that people are forced to settle in areas to the north and that people are subject to heavy *Islamization*. Sudanese Government spokesmen strongly deny these allegations and blame the unrest and the movement of people on the necessities of war.

This is not the place to go into detail on such issues. Nor is it the place to discuss whether this situation and the changes following in its wake will be short-term, to be reversed at the next coup in Khartoum; or long-term, through which basic elements of Sudanese society will change. At the time of sending this book to press they do, however, represent a context which is very different from the one during which most of this work was done, and it dramatizes some of the major themes I am dealing with.

When I started on the fieldwork in 1979 the general situation in the

Sudan was one of relative optimism. The country was putting the experiences of a long civil war behind it. The years following this war, which ended with the Addis Abeba Agreement in 1972, signalled the start of a period of reconstruction and development. Based on aid from Arab countries, Sudan set out to become the "Bread-basket of the Middle East". Agricultural development had highest priority and a number of large scale schemes were established to promote agricultural production. In the Nuba Mountains several mechanized schemes were started during this period, expanding grain and cotton production. Infrastructure was developed and general rural and urban development schemes established. Politically the period was one of nationbuilding and of the acceptance of pluralism. The political rhetoric emphasized the importance of "being Sudanese", belonging to "one nation" not to different "tribes", and so on.

During this period of development optimism, the universities in Bergen and Khartoum embarked upon a collaborative research effort. As a framework for this cooperation the *Savanna Project* was established. Starting in 1975, this joint research venture was concerned with analysing problems related to development and underdevelopment in the Sudan. Several studies were done, mainly in social anthropology, but also in economics and political science, on problems within traditional and modern agriculture and pastoralism focussing on labour migration, desert encroachment, mechanization of cultivation, local politics, trade and ethnicity. Such themes were studied within various empirical contexts of Western Sudan, Eastern and Central Sudan and the Ingessana region.

Although my study of the Nuba started in 1979, the theme with which I was concerned related closely to that earlier work within the Savanna Project. In 1976 I did one year's fieldwork in the Kheiran area of Northern Kordofan for my M.A. thesis. The Kheiran area consists of a series of small oases in which people engage in irrigated cultivation. The details are published in my book *The Sand Swallows Our Land* (Manger, 1981) but some of the general themes concern us here. The study focussed on the economic adaptations in that area and on the linkages between that oasis area and the surrounding villages on the savanna. My general interest was in the relationships between *intensive* and *extensive production systems* in this type of savanna area. This thematic interest also followed me in the Nuba Mountains. The mountains provided one of the relatively few areas within the Sudanese savanna areas in which intensification in the Boserup sense developed (Boserup, 1965). I was interested both in the methods of intensification, like the terracing of the mountain sides and manuring of fields, and in the organizational aspects like access to land and labour.

The applied aim of this work was to provide some insights to the many development plans and projects that had intensification of the savanna production systems as their explicit goal. One common characteristic of most of the plans and projects was that they were bringing new technologies for intensification from the outside. Tractors, ploughs and combined harvesters became a common sight in these scheme areas. Rather than look directly at such projects and development packages I was trying to find cases where intensification had developed within the indigeneous society itself. By looking at such cases the aim was to isolate factors that contributed to such developments and then bring back such lessons to decision makers dealing with agricultural development work. I have addressed such issues relating to savanna subsistence activities and the important parameters relating to productivity of land and labour in various publications (Manger 1980, 1981, 1987b, 1988, 1990). Although terms like "top-down planning" and "bottom-up approach" were not known to me when I started my work, and the emphasis on "indigeneous knowledge" was fairly rare among development planners, such catchwords may indicate the general areas to which my discussions were directed.

One overall trend of the arguments in these publications is that the emergence of intensive production systems in areas such as the Nuba Mountains are closely tied to the security situation there. New cultivation practices have developed historically, since slave raiding and other types of unrest forced certain people and groups to adopt to new environments in which they could protect themselves. Basic economic developments could, therefore, not be understood outside the context of the particular political history of the area. By some historical irony it is this second point which seems most relevant today. With the breakdown of security in the Nuba Mountains, following the expansion of the civil war, all development projects have ceased to function and the mountains may again provide some retreat for the Nuba populations to escape from rebel and government troops, as well as from the Baggara tribal militias (*murhalin*) and the Popular Defence Forces.

But the Nuba have not only been faced with threats to their physical and economic survival. Their survival as different cultural groups is also at stake. This issue, and the extent to which it was interwoven with the economic issues was less clear to me when I started my work in Liri. I was, of course, aware of the general historical context of the area and its inhabitants. But as I observed incidents that showed the important role this history played in defining the position of the Nuba within a wider society I became convinced that such processes are basic to our understanding of many development patterns in Nuba communities.

This understanding made it necessary to develop an argument in the context of the wider political history of the Nuba Mountains and also of the particular position the Nuba Mountains and similar areas (like the Ingessana and Dar Fertit) hold within the wider Sudanese society. People from these areas are called *zurqa*, i.e. blacks, and are regarded in a

Sudanese setting as not being proper Muslims. The reader will see how this type of reality helps shape some of the changes I analyse in this book. Processes conventionally labelled *Islamization* and *Arabization* thus took on far greater importance than I envisaged.

The political tensions inherent in these issues surfaced again in Sudanese politics in 1983, with President Nimeiri's introduction of the so-called September Laws. Islamic *sharia* law was given dominant status in the Sudanese legal system, also within the realm of criminal law. Seen from within Sudan, it was obvious from the beginning that this was a political move, meant to boost the president's weakened position. This was further underlined by giving the Muslim Brothers, or what is generally refered to as the Islamic Movement, a central political role. However, the effects were devastating. Not only did it end the era of optimism, but resulted, as we know, in political turmoil that swept Nimeiri's regime away in 1985 and further fuelled a civil war that might tear the country apart. An important element of the conflict is the definition of the Sudanese identity, and the application of the *sharia* dramatized to people of southern Sudan, as well as northern groups such as the Nuba that their identity was at stake and that their position as equal citizens in their country was far from settled.

However, as this book makes clear, the problem of integration for the Nuba did not originate in 1983. The eighteenth and nineteenth centuries represent periods of active pursuit of the Nuba for slaves. In this century the British colonial policy was aimed at isolating the Nuba and other groups from Arab and Muslim influence. This policy was based on a positive discrimination, but served as a stumbling block for later attempts at national integration. Following the independence of Sudan in 1956, there were attempts by the Nuba to create political organizations that could further their interests in the new national center. Thus in the 1960s the Central Union of the Nuba Mountains was established, alongside the Darfur Development Front and the Beja Congress to represent peripheral groups and to counteract the dominant position of the national parties, the Umma and DUP. With Nimeiri's take over in 1969, such organized political forces were disbanded. They were replaced by the Sudanese Socialist Union, a party and national force meant to bridge tribal and regional differences. The success at ending the civil war in 1972 and the ambitious development strategies actually provided considerable optimism. However, no real integration took place and the old elites remained dominant in Sudanese politics. And old attitudes did not die easily, as is aptly illustrated by the following quotation from Mansour Khalid, a key member of Nimeiri's regime from 1969 to 1978. He writes in his book *"The Government They Deserve: The Role of the Elite in Sudan's Political Evolution"*: "In the closed circles of northern Sudan there is a series of unprintable slurs for Sudanese of non-Arab stock, all reflective of semi-concealed prejudice" (1990:135).

The issue then, is how to compose a national identity in the Sudan in which not only Arabs and Muslims feel at home, but also non-Arabs and non-Muslims. As I worked on these issues, reading the available literature on Sudanese history and society I was struck by the extent to which the processes of Arabization and Islamization have been taken for granted in the history of that country. One basic assumption among Sudanese elites seems to be that this wave of socio-cultural change is a *natural* process and that it rolls of historical necessity from the "centers" in the Nile Valley towards the "peripheries" in eastern, western and southern Sudan. It follows that it is only a matter of time before the whole country is Arabized and Islamized. In this book I have a lot to say about such concepts and their analytic position in furthering our understanding of the Nuba. Here I only want to point at the fact that one tragic effect of such assumptions is that the political realities behind this spread of Arabism and Islam have not been dealt with in Sudanese politics. The problem is not one that can be isolated to the present regime and this civil war. Obviously the Islamists in Khartoum go further in expressing their intentions towards Arabization and Islamization than earlier regimes and they make no secret of their views of people who do not have this type of identity. The policies of the present regime thus dramatize the issue of *race* in Sudanese politics. But the issue of defining and constructing a Sudanese identity will not go away with this regime and, unless it is solved, the future for the Sudan looks bleak indeed.

My study of the Lafofa and my description of how they go about solving problems in their daily life may seem distant from these contemporary political processes. Yet I do think that the analysis of what went on in the Liri villages ten years ago shows clearly that the national problem, which I have refered to here, is in basic ways interlinked with microsociological processes in everyday Sudanese life. The relationship between such local processes and national party politics has not been a major concern of this study. But the analysis of how the Lafofa try to define an identity that allows them to participate in the social life of Liri clearly shows that the definition of a Sudanese identity is a problem that goes well beyond the realm of politics alone.

This book is built on my Ph.D. thesis (Dr. Philos) presented at the University of Bergen in March 1991. As the work on which it is based represents a period of more than ten years the number of people who have contributed with their thoughts, criticism and inspiration during this time is considerable. Several institutions have also been supportive and have contributed to my work at different times.

Professor Gunnar Håland and Director Gunnar Sørbø have both contributed in basic ways to my anthropological understanding and have at different stages provided valuable help. Gunnar Håland initiated the Savanna Project and formulated the ideas and hypotheses which made up an important context for my work. He also visited me in the field and has offered advice on many occasions since then. Gunnar Sørbø has also provided continous support. He has followed the writing of this book during most stages. His advice has always been valuable. In particular, his quick responses and constructive criticism of my various drafts towards the end, made the finishing of the book a lot easier. I gratefully acknowledge the support of both Gunnars. In Khartoum, Professor Abdul Ghaffar Mohamed Ahmed has been a key person of the Savanna Project. As a Director at the Social and Economic Research Council and later at the Development Studies and Research Center, he has always helped me in many ways, from assisting me to get research permits to providing academic advice as well as offering hospitality.

Many colleagues and friends in Bergen, Khartoum and elsewhere have made an input to this work. Fellow students on the Savanna Project, the "Group B" at the Department of Social Anthropology in Bergen (1979–86), staff at the Departments of Social Anthropology in Bergen and Khartoum, colleagues at the Center for Development Studies in Bergen, staff at the Social and Economic Research Council and the Development Studies and Research Center in Khartoum, the study teams of the Hunting Technical Services and the Western Sudan Agricultural Research Project in Kaduqli, staff at the Nuba Mountains Agricultural Production Corporation in Talodi and administrators in Kaduqli, Talodi and Liri have all helped me in various ways. Their names are too many to mention here but they know who they are and I thank them all.

In the critical finishing stages Professor Fredrik Barth provided encouragement for me to get on with it; Anwar Osman, assisted by the Media Center at the University of Bergen, helped to prepare the maps and various figures; and Anne Kari Håving, who earlier had typed much of the manuscript, also provided the final lay-out. Special mention should also be made of the two opponents of my Dr. Philos-thesis, Professor Ladislav Holy and Dr. Peter Loizos. They both offered valuable alternative viewpoints to my own argument and gave useful editorial advice. Professor Richard Pierce also helped a great deal, by improving my English as well as giving me general advice and encouragement.

This work could hardly have been undertaken without financial support from the Norwegian Agency for Development Cooperation (NORAD). They financed a three-year research grant (1979–82) as well as my different field trips, thus enabling me to continue my research interests in the Sudan. I also gratefully acknowledge financial support for earlier publications.

In Liri I am grateful for the help and friendship of Mohamed Koko

(Koeb'an), his family and the rest of the Lafofa villagers. I remember them telling me stories from the old days when their grandfathers escaped from different enemies, using their knowledge of every rock and cave in the hills as their weapon. Little did we know that soon they would need such knowledge and skills again. In Tunquro, *Haj* Ahmed, Abdel Galil, Hassan, Abdel Magid and the rest of the *suq* people did their utmost to help and allowed me to collect information on their lives and work. So did *Sheikh* Abdel Bagi Bernawi. Most of them have now moved away from Liri, but someday I hope we may meet there again with the rest of the "Lirawis". My thanks go to all of them.

Working on the Sudan and with the Sudanese for such a long time has left many marks on my personal life. My wife Karin and our two children, Ane and Åsmund, are witnesses to this, as they too have been strongly affected by my periodic physical and mental absenteeism. I thank them for tolerance, support and encouragement.

Map 1. *Map of the Sudan and Southern Kordofan*

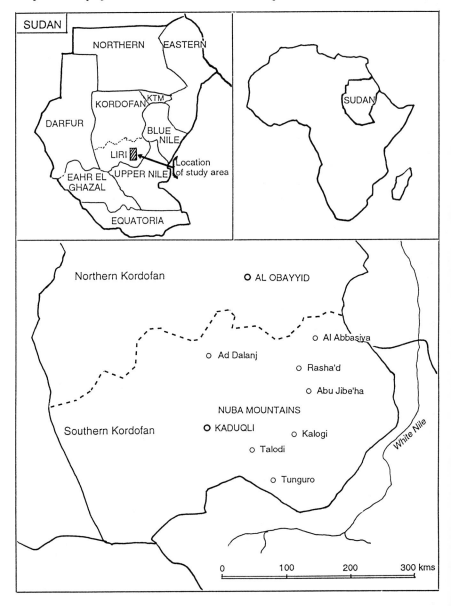

General introduction

> "Are the Lafofa moving forwards or backwards?"
> "FORWARDS!"
> "Then behave like Arabs, God Damn It!"

This exchange between a man and a crowd is taken from a local court session in the small Lafofa mountain village of Liri, a region in the very south of the Nuba Mountains in Central Sudan. The purpose of the court session was to reconcile two men who had a quarrel. The case itself is not important here. More interesting is the fact that the proceedings of the court case developed into a lot of quarreling, with people taking to the floor out of turn, some speaking in Arabic, some in Lafofa. This led to a heated discussion about what is proper behaviour, in court as well as in general. An Islamic Holy Man (*faqi*), who was brought to the mountain to bless the agreement, refused to do so. He would not bless "useless people" he said.

At this point a man jumped forward and gave a speech about proper behaviour. Nobody present could pretend they did not know about proper behaviour. They had been to the market on the plain, they had been to Khartoum, or their sons had been going there for many years, so they all knew. So why did they talk out of turn? And why did they not speak in Arabic in court? What would they do now, when they were refused the Islamic blessing? It was at this point that a man asked the question above, with great rhetorical drama, while the crowd responded by shouting their answer back.

This incident, small and insignificant as it seems, serves to bring us to the main topic of this book, which is a discussion of various socio-economic and socio-cultural changes among the Lafofa Nuba, following in the wake of their increased contact with the wider Sudanese society. Similar to most other Nuba groups, the contact is partly through a physical movement down from their mountain habitat to settle in the plains below, thus meeting other populations living there. Partly contact is through the general commercialization of their economy, with cash crop cultivation, local wage work and labour migration. But also in the political and administrative field, the affairs of the Nuba Mountains are to an increasing degree becoming affected by an expanding central government. Through participation in such activities, the Lafofa are becoming involved in social processes on a nationwide scale. Similarly, they are more exposed to influences from their Arab and Muslim neighbours, both through daily interaction as well as through a history of missionary activities.

The processes of change outlined above are discussed in the general literature under various headings like Arabization, Islamization, Sudanization, Commercialization and Modernization. They all represent major processes that indicate in which direction the integration of the Lafofa, and the Nuba in general, is moving. From being a pagan population, native to the Kordofanian plains, they have taken on many Arabic customs and adopted Arabic language. All Lafofa profess to be Muslims and they are becoming involved in a commercial economy like their Arabic and Muslim neighbours.

The implications of these changes are, however, different from one Nuba group to another. Regional variation in the historical processes of integration is one reason, differences in the social and cultural constitution of different Nuba groups is a second one. It is a major aim in this book to analyse and explain the direction of change as it appears among the Lafofa.

THE NUBA OF LIRI: SOME MAJOR CHANGES

The Lafofa is one of the groups living in Liri, the last market center in the Nuba Mountains as one travels southwards on the road from Kadugli towards the Upper Nile Province. In Liri there are also two other Nuba groups, the Liri Nuba and the Talasa Nuba. Compared to other Nuba groups (see e.g. Nadel, 1947; Faris, 1972; Stevenson, 1984; Salih, 1983; Baumann, 1987) the groups in Liri are small, and some of them are also immigrants to their present home areas. The Talasa Nuba is probably a branch of the Korongo who came to Liri around 1825–30. Their movement might have been due to a drought in the Tabuli area and they are today found in Liri and Kurindi (Stevenson, 1984). The Lafofa came as a result of the unrest in the southern Nuba Mountains during the Mahdia, i.e. the late 1880s. The Liri Nuba have been living in Liri, thus forming the only indigeneous Nuba group in the area.

The different origins of the groups also explain the fact that they speak different languages. The Liri speak a language which belongs to a subgroup of the Talodi-Masakin language group, Talasa is part of the Kadugli-Korongo language and Lafofa makes up a language group of its own together with the Amira Nuba to the south (Stevenson, 1984). All three languages are spoken today within the same mountain area, by people living within walking distance from each other. But in spite of the language differences several of the cultural characteristics of the three Nuba groups are similar and define the southern Nuba groups.

The Nuba populations in the southern parts make up groups of matrilineal people (Seligman, 1932; Nadel, op.cit.), the matrilineal principle being expressed in a descent ideology placing descendants together in the mother's line as a unolineal group. The kinship system is of a classificatory kind. All cousins are termed siblings, since father's and mother's siblings are classified as mothers and fathers. According to Seligman (ibid.) the lineages are shallow ones and relationships are not remembered for more than three generations.

Marriage was not a major ceremonial occasion. Young people arranged their own love affairs and if two people decided to marry they would tell their parents who would normally accept this. The link between the bridegroom and the bride's family was institutionalized in a bride service relationship. The wedding itself was a minor thing, although there was a party in which the drinking of beer was important.

The institutions that were important in regulating any person's life, and providing him or her with people to cooperate with, were not only found within the realm of the family and in-laws. In the daily life of a person the *age-mates* were also of great importance. There were seclusion ceremonies that took place shortly after puberty had been reached. Boys would spend the rainy season taking care of the cattle and they would live in cattle kraals. At the end of such a period of seclusion they would return and a ceremony would be performed. For girls, the transition ceremony implied seclusion in the granary, thus clearly bringing out the relationship between menstruation and female fertility, with that of the production of food for the reproduction of the groups as such. The age organization was not, however, elaborate and complex in the ways found elsewhere in the Nuba Mountains (see e.g. Nadel, 1947; Rottenburg, 1988).

A final institution that regulated people's lives was the existence of certain experts in the villages, called *kujor*. The most important of them was the rainmaker. He was a man of great dignity, possessing powers from the ancestors to bring the rain that is so crucial for cultivation. For his services to the community, the rainmaker had his plot cultivated for him, and was also paid in beer. Apart from the rainmaker, there were departmental experts who operated along the same principles. There were experts for each of the important crops. Sickness experts were also important, as they could cure people through their powers. And finally, there was an iron expert. A common way of paying all these experts was in beer.

The general framework of the social organization outlined above has undergone changes through the decades of this century. The matrilineal principle is still there, but it is not as critical an organizational principle as it used to be. Marriage is totally changed, now being penetrated by Arabic customs and being ruled by Islamic *sharia* principles. The position of the rainmaker and other experts is challenged by Islamic holy men, who perform the same functions, relating their powers to Allah instead of their ancestors. The age grade system is no longer a living institution among the Nuba of the southern mountains and the seclusion periods no longer exist.

Today the transition ceremonies are the Islamic ones, i.e. namesgiving, circumcision (of both girls and boys) and marriage. The ceremonies are individual and the Islamic holy men provide the blessing. At the death of a person he or she is buried in individual graves, not in the former lineage graves. The cermony is Islamic, with a seven days mourning period.

DEVELOPMENTS PRODUCING CHANGE

The above changes must be seen against the background of an increasing integration of the Nuba groups into Sudanese society at large. Through such processes, they have been exposed to new socio-economic forms, new behavioural patterns and new religious thoughts and activities. However, such processes of integration are *localized* and should not be generalized to apply to all the Nuba. In Liri the history of contacts differs between the three Nuba groups there and I shall, therefore, return to and concentrate on the Lafofa story.

At the turn of the century the Lafofa were living in a mountain village on the Liri mountain. There they practiced a quite intensive system of cultivation with the multiple linkages between agriculture and livestock and labour demanding dry terracing. This intensive cultivation evolved in the context of population pressure on the confined mountain plateau. But this agricultural system was also the focal point around which many rituals and ceremonies of importance to the Lafofa revolved. During the years of this century this system has changed significantly.

The Lafofa have to a large extent left their mountain habitat and are now living in several villages down on the Liri plain. This down-movement happened as a result of a serious conflict with the British. The Lafofa were, therefore, forced to settle on the plain in 1930, and only later could they start moving up the mountain again. The majority, however, stayed on the plain.

This down-movement has led to a change from intensive hill cultivation to a more extensive cultivation, in which the fields on the plain become economically more significant than the smaller fields on the mountain. When the security situation made cultivation in the plains possible, the pressure on resources was significantly reduced and the Lafofa adopted a less labour-intensive cultivation system. Today the Lafofa's most important fields are out on the clay plains where they cultivate together with the rest of the population of the region. This is true for the people in the mountain village as well as for those now settled in plain villages. The crops cultivated are sorghum and peanuts, the latter as cash crops. Cultivation of cash crops and the shift from the mountain fields to fields on the plain are thus two important developments characterizing the integration process.

This change has made access to land less problematic, as far field-land is still in abundance in Liri. Wage labour is increasing in importance as traditional communal work groups, that were so important in the intensive system, lose their function. New patterns of economic differentiation appear to be based on availability of cash. But most importantly, with the changing agricultural system, the localized matrilineal descent groups were scattered and important rituals related to the agricultural cycle were changed. With this, important elements in the reproduction of the Lafofa cultural tradition also changed.

Another important change is the Lafofa involvement in labour migration to the Khartoum area. Compared to other groups in the area such migration among the Lafofa started rather late, in the 1960's, coinciding with an expanding national industry in Khartoum. This particular history of migration has resulted in a clear pattern among the Lafofa men, in which those over about 50 years of age have never been on migration, whereas those who are younger have made at least one trip. Today migration is an essential part of the process of a young Lafofa man establishing himself with a wife and family. Many continue to migrate, making this migration and the money brought from it an integral part of the local economy of contemporary Lafofa.

Among the women there is no clear differentiation in economic activities, but there are differences in the extent to which they adopt a lifestyle based on Sudanese standards. There is also a difference between older and younger women in this respect; the younger ones adapting to the Sudanese ideals about a woman's appearance, behaviour and involvement in socio-economic life. Furthermore, the economic units are changing. Earlier the individual spouses made up a production unit, whereas in the contemporary context there is a development towards joint households. Relations within the units, i.e. relations between the sexes, are also changing, the women becoming more dependent on the men. New patterns of local differentiation are also emerging, as cash invested in local cultivation opens up new possibilities for those Lafofa who control such cash.

Changes within the socio-cultural level are also, as we said at the beginning, tied to processes of Arabization and Islamization. The down-movement brought the Lafofa into direct contact with the other groups living in Liri, most of them of Arabic origin. Unlike areas further north in the mountains (e.g. the Miri, see Baumann, 1987) there has been no large influx of Lafofa slaves bringing back Islam and Arabic customs from their period of captivity.

In Liri it was the activities of Islamic missionaries that brought the influences producing changes in the social organization of the Lafofa as well as in the basic notions they hold about the world and their place in it. Such missionaries are the members of various *sufi* brotherhoods, most importantly the Qadiriyya. As a result of all these processes, the very content of "being Lafofa" has changed and people today think and behave in significantly different ways from what they did only a generation ago.

DIFFERENTIATED CHANGE

It is one important premise for the discussion of the Lafofa in this book that the processes of change sketched out above are not uniform, nor do they affect all Lafofa in the same way. For instance, while doing fieldwork I could clearly see how young men involved in labour migration and local trade were much more inclined to present Islamic identities and to argue for the necessity of adopting Arabic customs, than were the old-timers.

Likewise, among the women, the wives of these migrants showed similar characteristics when compared to their older sisters. The ways of old people are "backwards" they said, and they still hold on to their "superstitious" beliefs. Such observations may not be surprising when we see the different economic and social strategies these various groups of Lafofa are following. One of my aims is thus to show how some Lafofa, by becoming involved in new economic strategies, not only have created new economic realities for themselves, but also come to act as agents of change to produce new socio-cultural realities for all Lafofa.

The changes are thus clearly tied to the *degree of mobility* among different categories of people. Young Lafofa, when reaching out from their local communities become exposed to and must deal with wider socio-cultural environments than was the case before. To participate in meaningful ways, they have to present social identities that are acceptable to this wider environment.

As the Lafofa, and the Nuba in general, are considered a former *slave population* with a *stigma* on their identity, this process of social adaptation becomes particularly crucial. The ways different categories of people deal with this stigma is an important factor explaining differentiated behaviour among the Nuba themselves, how networks are established and how they relate to the outside world. This internal variation provides an entry into the actual processes by which wider cultural variation occurs.

THE NUBA WITHIN A WIDER SOCIAL FIELD

The problem relates to the general history of the Nuba Mountains as a frontier region. This frontier was a field of economic and human exploitation through raiding and slaving. It was also a zone where ethnic and societal transformations took place, often as a consequence of assumptions of inferiority and superiority, assumptions reinforced by religion and assumed descent (O'Fahey, 1982:1).

Although this happened throughout the whole Nuba Mountains area (as it did in other frontier regions like Ingessana and Dar Fertit) the history of the southern Nuba Mountains is somewhat special. It has to do with the region's position deep in the mountains, making it into a haven for run-away slaves (Hargey, 1981). Many serf-like communities were also found there, in which slaves adopted the tribal identities of their former masters. The history of unrest brought about by punitive expeditions towards the Nuba by Mahdist troops in the late 1880s, also brought about dramatic resettlements in the region.

The migration of the Lafofa reflects this history, as does the presence of former Nuba slaves who now live in Liri and who have taken on the identities of Hawazma Arabs. The same developments occured in Talodi and Kalogi; the slaves there taking on the identity of their Messiriyya and Kawahla masters respectively.

In this century, the area has seen an influx of *jellaba* traders, West African *fellata* and Southerners (Dinka, Nuer, Shilluk). This is due to the opening up of the mountains for commercial activities and the availability of wage work that followed. It is also the result of the British use of force, such as the Lafofa incidence in 1930, that resulted in forced down-movement of people from their hills. As a consequence of all this, the localities around the market centers in this region are highly complex in their ethnic and cultural composition. It is to this complex local scene that the Lafofa expose themselves when leaving the mountain.

The evolving relations between such groups are not only defined by the local Liri scene but also by the position of the various groups in the wider Sudanese social context. The main factor influencing this is that of the social power carried by participants in the local arenas of interaction like Liri. Comparing the Nuba with the Arab populations, this distribution of power is clearly in favour of the Arabic groups, against the non-Arabs and non-Muslims. This is related to the long history of Arabization and Islamization in the Sudan, through which local groups have adopted new cultural traits. Many societies went through this process centuries ago, but for the Nuba Mountains and the Liri region it is a contemporary process and the presentation of behaviour that can be accepted within that Arabic and Islamic code is necessary.

In addition, there is a contemporary process of change going on in the Sudan. This process of social change is not one of accepting the Islamic religion or Arabic language and customs alone, but rather, that ethnically diverse groups living on the Sudanese periphery, adapt to the dominant life-style of the centre. Non-Arab and non-Islamized groups like the Nuba show the most dramatic expression of such processes, but Arab groups already Islamized are also going through similar processes. This process does not mean that people only want to catch up with the mainstream Arabic culture, but rather, "materially and spiritually to participate as a member of the Sudanese top stratum of traders and officials, and to be taken seriously, be considered trust and creditworthy throughout the Sudan" (Doornbos, 1984).

This is a general process of social change going on in contemporary Sudan, and it is a complex phenomenon related to different agents of social change. Traders are among the major agents of this change; so are modern schools, local courts and Islamic brotherhoods. This way of life is characterized by non-manual labour, non-drinking, seclusion of women, a clear public display of Islamic identity (Doornbos, op.cit.).

In Liri the *jellaba* represent such a way of life while the Nuba represent the opposite of this. The Nuba are still considered a non-Muslim, non-Arab population, with a past history as slaves, and they are still marginal to society. Together with some other groups like the Ingessana, they make up what is called the *zuruq* (the blacks) which is a derogatory term. These groups suffered particular harassment in Sudanese towns during the final years of the Nimeiri regime, when *sharia* law was most actively applied. Also in the socio-economic field they are mostly at the bottom, serving as cheap labour in urban industries, being domestic servants or working as casual labour. An important point to understand the Lafofa, as they participate in the plural Liri scene, is that there is a *stigma* on their identity with which they have to deal, if they want to participate fully on that scene.

THE EMERGENCE OF NEW ECONOMIC OPPORTUNITIES

This state of affairs is further affected by the fact that the economic situation in the Sudan is changing, which creates new opportunities and constraints for the participants. This is related to the process of commercialization of the Sudanese economy.

The increase in the rate of commercialization is an ongoing process in the Sudan and it manifests itself at various levels. Local farmers and pastoralists are, to an increasing degree, becoming involved in the market sector through buying consumer goods and the selling of crops and animals. In contemporary Sudan the very reproduction of rural communities is dependent on this market link. Cash crops are being cultivated at an increasing rate. One expression of the increasing importance of the commercial link is that the traditional subsistence crop, sorghum, has become the major cash crop in many areas.

In Liri, sorghum is today more important as a cash crop than the "traditional" ones of peanuts and cotton. Alongside the involvement in cash-crops, there is also an involvement in wage labour, either locally or through migration. In Southern Kordofan, of which Liri is a part, the establishment of mechanized schemes has created new opportunities for wage labour close to where people live, and has become an alternative to long-distance migration to the Nile Valley. The incomes from wage labour are today not only an additional source of income for the families but a crucial input factor in local cultivation, as wage incomes are spent locally on mobilizing labourers to expand their own cultivation.

A second expression of the increasing rate of commercialization is seen in the expanding trade sector. Indigeneous trade in the Sudan has traditionally been dominated by the *jellaba* traders from the Nile Valley. Their command of capital, organizational skills and links to the political field made them superior in solving problems inherent in trade. In recent decades, however, new and more profitable options have opened up for these groups. Investments in mechanized scheme-farming, as is happening in Liri, is a case in point. Involvement in export–import trade, investments in urban housing are other examples of strategies that have made the *jellaba* leave their involvement in the consumer trade (Manger, 1984).

This has opened up a new field of investment for the people who have success in their own traditional adaptation. A good cash crop or incomes from wages help people to create small surpluses. The most common way to invest small surpluses is in petty trading, and many people are doing that. Further success can now be converted into increased trade in consumer goods and the operation of a permanent shop.

The general picture then, is no longer a simple dichotomy of subsistence oriented farmers and pastoralists versus the *jellaba* commercial groups, who are the main agents of commercialization. It is rather a complex setting in which most groups have become deeply involved in the commercial process and are looking for investment opportunities to further improve their position.

The interplay between such processes of commercialization, which open new economic possibilities for people, and the requirements these opportunities make of people to follow specific identity management strategies, serve as important contexts for our further discussion. This is particularly true for the Nuba, who, as we said, have a stigma on their identity. In this respect the Nuba held a marginal position, whereas the Arabs, and particularly the *jellaba* traders, make up a social and cultural majority. To some extent, then, one important dynamic of social change among the Lafofa must be sought in this identity game, which is a strategic adaptation of some Lafofa to new environments, in which a primary aim is to overcome a marginal social position.

The acceptance that they themselves have an inferior social status in the wider stratificational system of the Sudan, thus brings about a process of *emulation*. But this is not new to the Lafofa. All through this century, the gradual integration of this particular group into society at large has produced similar problems, leading to processes of ethnic dichotomization. The difference is that today this integration process is more penetrating than it was before. By the overall commercialization in the Sudan and the increasing degree of labour migration, the exposure to, and the need to relate to other groups in a continuous manner has increased. But this is a matter of degree, not of quality, and the overall effect has been one of the Lafofa adopting foreign ways of life.

DYNAMICS OF CHANGE AMONG THE LAFOFA

For a long time then the Lafofa have been involved in an interactional game in which they have used signs and symbols to show an Arabic and Muslim environment that they are human beings, that they are respectable persons and not slaves and pagans. This process of ethnic dichotomization has also had important repercussions on the Lafofa's cultural traditions. We have outlined some general changes in social organization, but also notions of physical and sexual shame have changed and so have their transition ceremonies. Food taboos have changed, as have notions of gender relations, to mention but a few. Another important aim of the book is, therefore, to show how those individual strategies relating to Lafofa identity management produce results than can be termed cultural change.

To do this, we have to return to the differences in the ways individual Lafofa are involved in contact with other groups. Through different economic strategies some people become much exposed, for instance, through labour migration or local trade. Others, who are only involved in local cultivation, have much less of a need to expose themselves to this environment.

I assume here that culture is part of a person and has to be enacted not only comprehended. This means that the ideas that make up a culture must develop in each individual person as a result of continuous experiences throughout life. People with similar experiences will therefore develop similarities in their outlook on the world (Barth, 1983). In order to understand the emergence and maintenance of cultural differences among the Lafofa, we should, therefore, look at the processes affecting the social identities among the Lafofa. This opens the way for an analysis of how the differences in exposure of various groups of Lafofa to the external world, create differences in their outlook on the world.

Such new outlooks also become relevant among the Lafofa themselves. The Lafofa interact and live out what we may call the Lafofa culture. But this "culture" will mean different things to different participants, given the differences in their relations to the external world. If it is true that "man is an animal suspended in webs of significance he himself has spun" (Geertz, 1973:5) different groups of Lafofa will *confer* different meanings on to their existence. We shall see that migrants do things differently from older men, that there are differences between younger and older women, between people holding traditional positions, like the traditional ritual experts, and new converts to Islam.

The ways such meanings are conferred on the world can be observed in encounters of interaction and we can thus observe how various types of signs are used to express such variation among the Lafofa. The analysis of such encounters, and how different people participate in such encounters, may thus lead us on to the processes that form the basis for the development of new notions about the world. This is so because such encounters contain communicative messages expressed by the actors.

By comparing descriptions of such encounters, we may uncover important dynamics in the reproduction of "traditional" elements of Lafofa culture, as well as seeing how new elements may replace them, thus leading to change. I shall argue that the changes outlined may be described as the outcome of changes in important encounters in which basic sociocultural relationships and their content are being expressed. Changes in such encounters also imply changes in the messages that are communicated, and thus form a basis for the development of new notions about the world.

It is, however, important to note that we are not talking about a change from a unified, traditional Lafofa culture into a more disintegrated one, with new elements existing along with old ones.

What I have called "traditional" Lafofa culture is not altogether gone, nor have old people living a "traditional" life dissappeared. But with the emergence of new adaptive opportunities, the complexity of Lafofa adaptation has increased and new "agents of change" have entered the scene. A major aim is, therefore, also to try to uncover the processes affecting the reproduction and change of the Lafofa culture, a task which clearly not only involves a need to understand major aspects of how the Lafofa culture is constituted, but also how new elements have been adopted and have affected processes of reproduction and change.

AN ANALYTICAL OUTLINE

The processes of change and assimilation illustrated by the above presentation are discussed in the general literature under various headings like Arabization, Islamization and Sudanization (for the Nuba Mountains see e.g. Nadel, 1947; Stevenson, 1966; Baumann, 1987. For similar processes among other groups in the Sudan see e.g. James, 1971; Jedrej, 1974; Doornbos, 1984). The issue of change also occurs in debates in Indian ethnography about the value of Sanscritization as an analytical tool to understand social change in India. As the lower castes of India seek a higher social status, they emulate the life-styles of higher castes; Sanscritization thus becoming a process of social mobility through elite emulation (see e.g. Srinivas, 1967 and Carroll, 1977).

The same perspective is used for changes among tribal groups in India (e.g. Orans, 1965). In the same way, we may see the Nuba emulating the life-styles of the dominant Arab and Muslim groups, thus trying to change a marginal and stigmatized identity into a socially acceptable one. There are, however, several analytical points to be made about the use of concepts such as the ones mentioned above. The terms are frequently used with the implied assumption that they represent the goal towards which integration processes among the Nuba are moving. But one problem is to what extent such broad descriptive terms help to understand the underlying processes of change.

Assuming unity of culture

One problem with approaching the process of integration through such descriptive labelling is that we may be led to see the process of change as having a uniform momentum towards a set horizon of Islamic, Arabic and Sudanese customs and values. The research task then often becomes to measure the state reached by a certain community, e.g. the Lafofa, on the road towards these horizons, ranking them according to how far they have "developed" towards them from the "traditional". Although there is nothing wrong with descriptions of how socio-cultural features have changed over time, we are, however, facing a great methodological difficulty when we try to "explain" such developments.

One set of problems is how we conceptualize society and culture. Relating to the field of Nuba studies, a commonly held view in earlier literature (e.g. Nadel, 1947; Stevenson, 1967) is based on conceptualising culture and society as logically integrated systems of structures and ideas. When confronted with other types of societies and cultural systems, the original systems "adopt" various ideas and forms from them and such elements are integrated into the old socio-cultural system. From this perspective, one may try to "explain" the diffusion of specific features from one "culture" or one "society" to another.

I do, however, find it difficult to understand how such a perspective on incremental integrated borrowing can produce changes in the logic of integration, i.e. fundamental social and cultural change, which the end result of the process must imply. In my view, it is not fruitful to seek answers about the changes among the Lafofa by comparing a total Lafofa socio-cultural and socio-economic system to an Arab or Sudanese one. This is because we can not delineate such an integrated unit with clear boundaries. Empirically, we see that the Lafofa perform and utilise a complexity of customs, rituals and symbols, and it would be extremely difficult to meaningfully classify some as traditional Lafofa and others as Sudanese.

An even greater difficulty would be to construct the inter-connected-ness between such elements and thereby establish the integration of such a new system. The only way to handle this is not to look for such an integration at all but to see society and culture as a collection of practices, symbols and codes that are made use of in situations of interaction. People take up new practices and leave others, new signs are created as old ones go out of use, not so much as part of a planned process but as a result of the situations within which people operate in a wider social context.

An important starting point for our analysis is, therefore, to look at the participation of the Lafofa in various arenas and situations and to try to identify the activities and the symbols they make use of and the cultural codes and values they refer to, to justify their position and arguments.

This is not to say that there is no integration. Certainly, signs and symbols can be related into meaningful wholes, and also related to other fields of social and economic life. But such inter-relationships *must be discovered*, and *documented empirically*, they can not be assumed a priori, as following from some logical necessity.

Economy, politics and culture as part of daily life

This refers to another weakness with the terms used above; they lead to assumptions that the processes of change occuring in each of them are unrelated to those in another one. With this kind of reasoning, Arabization and Islamization would relate to a discussion of social organization, customs and culture, and commercialization would have to do with the economic level of society. One important point in this thesis is, however, that they are closely related and that it is precisely in the way they are inter-related that the dynamics of change can be sought. An analysis of how symbols are destroyed or created as discussed above must, therefore, be tied to other aspects of interaction and the socio-economic and socio-political life. Economic life, agriculture, political and administrative realities, which are all part of the integration process for the Lafofa, must, therefore, not only be depicted as general contexts but as *part of daily life*, i.e. as parts of one and the same empirical process.

This point is similar to the way Keesing used the term "political economy of meaning" (Keesing, 1982) to say that those symbols and meanings that make up a culture are certainly situated in individual minds, but they are *realized* in social and political contexts of everyday life.

Fredrik Barth (1982, 1983, 1987) takes a similar view, emphasizing that cultural traditions are shared, embraced and transmitted by persons with a common social identity (see Barth, 1983:193). Culture to Barth is part of a person, and has to be enacted, not only comprehended. This means that the ideas that make up a culture must develop in each individual person as a result of continuous experience through life, and consequently that people with similar experiences will develop similarities in their outlook on the world. But again, this does not mean that new values and outlooks on life are totally shared by everybody. Values may not be coherent, even if they are shared (Barth, 1989:7). But still, such values affect people's choices and actions, as they function as conceptual underpinnings that enhance or generate socially desirable behaviour. This will vary in different cultures at different times and such changes can be established (Barth, ibid.:14).

This does not mean that we can reduce culture to a study of individuals. Reproduction of culture obviously depends on a collective social process. My argument is, however, that individuals are carriers of culture and through their activities they help reproduce culture. What individuals do and think is, therefore, an important starting point for this line of thinking.

I have emphasized distinctions between migrants, and the old-timers. We could do the same by focusing on gender, how differences in outlook on life differ between men and women. Or we could pursue differences in knowledge between ritual experts and common people. We could then establish a pattern in which culture is seen as being distributed among members of a society. The way such people participate, and make use of their cultural inventories in specific situations, for specific purposes, provides important information for understanding change.

Cultural content and direction of change

A third problem relates to how we can understand the *direction* of change, and at what level of social life such changes occur. One concept, that is used in discussions of processes of the kind we are dealing with, is that of *assimilation*. In a recent monograph, on the Miri Nuba, Gerd Baumann (1987) points to one aspect of this problem. He critizises Sigfried Nadel's usage of *assimilation* in his classical book on the Nuba (1947), for lumping together many processes and assuming they were of the same kind. This discussion of assimilation is found in the final chapter of Nadel's book, in which he discusses aspects of processes of integration among the Nuba. He argues that the ultimate assimilation of the Nuba would only occur when intermarrying was established between Nuba and Arabs. Only then would the Nuba children come under the influence of Arab thought and ways of life (Nadel, 1947:488–89). However, as we shall see in this thesis, the general integration of Nuba groups into society at large has created profound economic and socio-cultural changes, although intermarrying between Nubas and Arabs is not yet very common.

The reason Nadel argued the way he did, as interpreted by Baumann and I agree, is a consequence of his lumping together of Arabization, Islamization as well as borrowing from other Nuba groups. He thus regarded Arabization and Islamization as parallel to other types of cultural borrowing, for instance between Nuba groups themselves. This view does not take into account the force of those integrative processes that are supported by society at large, including the State itself. Putting the Nuba in the wider perspective of national development processes, a national system of stratification and of public policies of education and religious life will show that the processes of Arabization and Islamization, and of the contemporary one that I call "Sudanization" are of a different nature than local borrowing between groups.

Baumann goes on to discuss how the Miri, in spite of the processes they are involved in, maintain a unity. Baumann introduces the concept of "redintegration," defined as "to restore to a state of wholeness, completeness, or unity; to renew, re-establish, in a united or perfect state" to explain this (Baumann, 1987:3). But Baumann relates his discussion to how *social categories* are being reproduced, thus relating to the literature on ethnicity.

For the purposes of this thesis, however, we need concepts that lead our attention on to *cultural content*, without assuming changes in ethnic and social identities. The developments outlined in this introduction have certainly lead to a reduction in the distinctiveness of Lafofa culture. What I see is a continous emptying of traditional Lafofa symbols of their meanings and "traditional" values, beliefs and expressions are classified as "superstition" and "backwardness" in the process.

But the changes I am talking about are not changing the Lafofa as a social category in Liri. All people who are born Lafofa still consider themselves to be members of that group, in spite of the stigma on their identity. To understand this, we need to look for concepts that allow us to differentiate between developments affecting social identities and those affecting cultural content.

I shall try to solve this by introducing the old concepts of the Great Tradition and Little Tradition (Marriott, 1955), in which the focus is on the reproduction of culture. The Lafofa thus appear to have a Little Tradition that is in contact with an Arabic/Islamic/Sudanese Great Tradition. The processes we are concerned with are those of *parochialization*, i.e. how ideas from the Great Tradition are adopted and become part of the Little Tradition. As in the Indian case, part of this is through a literate elite, trained within a certain tradition of knowledge, meeting a local, orally based tradition. Marriott depicts the resulting interaction as a *channel of communication* in which "specialists" from the two traditions interact. Focusing on situations of interaction provides clues to understanding the change itself. In anthropological literature much attention has been paid to rituals and how they provide new insights for the participants. But I think we can use the same perspective to view everyday interaction, and

ask questions like: what is being created in interaction? what is being communicated? and, which metaphors are used?

In the Lafofa case, an important point is that the resulting social
change is not random, but is dependent on the wider social context. The
dynamic and direction of change depends on how people are involved in
different activites, and how they pursue different strategies within systems on different levels of scale. Since this participation depends on economic assets as well as socio-cultural competence, including dealing with
a social stigma, the end result is dependent on how people handle this
situation: it must be seen as a *process of management*. With that, we have returned to individual people being the important link between local processes and processes on a macro-scale. People participate, and this affects
processes of status-summation, i.e. the content of being a Lafofa social
person. The inter-relationship between these different levels must also
be established empirically.

FIELDWORK AND METHODOLOGY

The fieldwork on which this study is based was undertaken in four different periods. My first visit to the area was from March to June 1979. Then
I travelled around in the southern Nuba Mountains area to get an impression of its geography and people. My base during this first visit was with
the Nuba Mountains Agricultural Production Corporation in Talodi.
The executives there told me a lot about their work on the cotton
schemes, and their understanding of the economic system in the area
later proved helpful.

From Talodi I moved on to Liri. I did this for two reasons: firstly because I had information that there were people living in villages up in the
mountains proper. The villages I had visited were mainly on the slopes of
hills or out on the plain. Secondly, there was a community of merchants
involved in the cultivation of sorghum on mechanized schemes. This
could bring me into a regional pattern of differentiation and it would
provide information on a very important sector of the Government's
policy of rural development, i.e. the establishment of mechanized
schemes.

After visiting the Lafofa and Liri villages up on the mountain, I decided to stay in the area and make Liri my base for intensive fieldwork. I
stayed there, mainly on the mountain, until June 1979, getting to know
people, collecting as much information as I could, while participating in
the daily lives of people. I also established contact with the merchants in
the market places and started to look into their activities.

When I left the field in June I stopped in Dilling on my way back to
Khartoum. In Dilling I visited the offices of Sudan's Agricultural Bank

and The Mechanized Farming Corporation, both of which play central parts in the development schemes in the Nuba Mountains.

My second period of fieldwork was from late September 1979 to March 1980. Most of the time I spent in the Lafofa village up on the mountain, but I also visited some plain villages with Lafofa inhabitants, among them being *Um Gudja* where Lafofa from the mountain have settled to be closer to their far fields. I also went to *al Baida*, the scheme, to collect information on cultivation. On visits to the regional towns I continued to visit public offices to get as much information as possible.

A third period of fieldwork was undertaken during a three month stay, from April until July 1981. During this time I checked much of the information I had collected earlier about mountain adaptation. I followed the merchants on their marketing trips of the *Baida* grain to Southern Sudan and I continued "to haunt" the public offices in the area.

During my last stay, March–June 1984, I was more into the problem of general socio-cultural change. I stayed in the market town of Tunguru to get a wider data-base for understanding the changes I had observed on the mountain.

When I came to the field I had a fair knowledge of Arabic and among Arabic speakers I was able to work without having an interpreter all the time. The Lafofa, who speak their own native tongue among themselves, also know Arabic. It was a drawback that I was unable to learn enough Lafofa to speak it. I was, therefore, dependent on having conversations translated into Arabic. I never used any specific interpreter but asked people who were there to translate. As I became friends with the people this did not provide any difficulty and I could spend a considerable time after an event talking to a participant to get his version of what had happened. I could then refer to such events later on and get an impression of what other people thought about it.

The main approach of my fieldwork was participant-observation. This approach gives the researcher the possibility of getting to know people and doing research at the same time. Censuses, more formal interviews and the taking of photographs, did not create problems as far as I can judge. Through these formal methods I mapped the communities out in terms of households, kinship, sources of income, tribal membership and the history of the area.

THE ORGANIZATION OF THIS BOOK

To carry out an analysis of the type described in the General Introduction, I have organized my material and my discussion in the following way.

Chapter 1 contains a general presentation of the Liri region. The various groups living there are presented and so are the histories of settlement that brought them there. I also concentrate on the ways Liri gradually has become an integral part of the administrative, economic and cultural life of the southern Nuba Mountains and of the Sudanese nation. The discussion consists of historical sketches that are meant to provide a background for understanding the regional game the Lafofa enter when coming down from the mountain. It is also a first presentation of a region that has not previously been dealt with within the field of Nuba studies.

In Chapter 2, I begin the discussion relating specifically to the Lafofa. In this chapter, my aim is to describe basic aspects of Lafofa culture and society, as it was observed in the early parts of this century. Descent and kinship are discussed, as are other elements of social organization, like transition ceremonies and major forms of ritual life. Local cultivation is also described, and the ways local cultivation and other levels of Lafofa social and cultural life are interrelated is shown.

Chapter 3 focuses on contemporary Lafofa society and is a description of the type of society that met the ethnographer during fieldwork. The chapter shows how the earlier system has been transformed, not as a uniform process of change, but rather as different elements showing different tendencies of change. The direction of change is, however, one towards Arabized and Islamized customs and type of behaviour.

Chapter 4 shows how these changes, both in the socio-cultural and in the economic fields, have affected the households, or economic units among the Lafofa. The integration of the Lafofa into a wider society has produced a variety of adaptive strategies among the Lafofa. Due to the integration, important changes have occured, affecting the constitution of the economic unit, both its establishment through marriage and its maintenance. Through a number of case studies, I shall show how such changes have affected the different ways in which Lafofa economic units adapt.

Chapter 5 goes on to present an analysis of how different adaptive strategies work and affect local economic differentiation among the Lafofa. We shall see in particular how those units with members engaging in labour migration over long periods acquire a better economic position than do those who concentrate on local cultivation and the keeping of animals. By providing detailed discussions of the management processes of Lafofa units, I try to show how economic differences emerge within the group. Although some Lafofa stand out as being more successful in economic life than others, they all remain at the bottom of the regional system of differentiation in Liri. Their economic success is insignificant when compared to the groups that represent the top of this ladder, particularly the *jellaba* group.

Chapter 6 focuses on another aspect of the integration of the Lafofa into society at large. The focus is on the Liri region and what it implies for the Lafofa to participate in that plural region. The aim is to show how the region is dominated by groups with Arabic and Islamic backgrounds and values. Interaction in Liri is, thus, to an important extent defined by such groups, and groups with non-Arabic, an$ non-Islamic background must deal with this. I show what it implies for the Lafofa to participate in this plural context, thus relating the processes of Arabization and Islamization within one group to wider socio-economic and interactional processes in the region as well as in the Sudan. I then take the lessons learned about how different Lafofa deal with interaction in Liri as a point of departure for discussing the dynamics of change observed in local cultivation, particularly with reference to communal work groups. Important changes in this field can be understood only against the background of the Lafofa migrants trying to build new identities for themselves, so that they may be accepted in a wider social context.

Finally, Chapter 7 sums up the major empirical changes we have been discussing and elaborates on the dynamics of change. The theoretical lessons and implications from this discussion are pointed out and related to the analytical comments presented in the General Introduction.

1. The Liri region: Some historical trends

Liri is on the main road that runs southwards from Kadugli and Talodi through Liri towards Tunga on the White Nile. It is the last market-center before one leaves South Kordofan to enter the Upper Nile Province. When travelling to Liri by car along the main road from Talodi one arrives at the Liri Mountain at its north-western end. During the final kilometers, one passes through numerous villages that are spread along the mountain. Finally one enters the Liri market place, which is called Tunguru.

If the trip were to continue, a similar pattern of villages would emerge south of Tunguru. A series of villages is situated along the mountainside, turning eastwards with the mountain, continuing on the eastern side. On the eastern side there is also a market center, called *al Khor*, due east of Tunguru. Up on the mountain itself, not visible from the plain, and accessible only after a short climb up the mountain, are two more villages, situated on two different mountain plains. When walking from Tunguru to al Khor, along the path crossing the mountain, one would pass through one of them, Lafofa, but to reach the second one called Liri, one would have to make a further climb. This pattern of settlements is shown in Map 2, while Map 3 gives an overview of Tunguru.

THE LIRI REGION

The inhabitants belong to different ethnic groups. The Arabs of Liri are of Hawazma and Kawahla stock, whereas the Nuba come from three different groups, the Liri, the Talasa and the Lafofa. In addition to these groups, members of the *jellaba* trading community are living in the two market towns in the area and there are some West Africans (*fellata*) and some Southerners (Nuer, Dinka and Shilluk).

Farmers and pastoralists

In ecological terms, the southern Nuba Mountains area has several mountains and hills, separated by wide plains of sand and clay soils. The general geographical area I deal with is the triangle between the three towns and market centres of Talodi, Kalogi and El Liri (see Map 4). Liri, the southernmost of these mountains, is surrounded by areas of sandy soil. Further away one enters the clay plains so characteristic of southern

Table 1. *Liri villages and tribal affiliation of inhabitants*

Villages	Tribal groups
Serref	Hawazma/Rawauga (Delemia)
Um Kwaro	Hawazma/Rawauga (Dar Gama'i)
Tera	Hawazma/Rawauga (Delemia)
Talo	Hawazma/Rawauga (Awlad Nuba), fellata/Takarir
Jorrob	Lafofa Nuba
Tunguru	Hawazma/Abd el-Ali (Dar Gawad, Awlad Ghabosh, Dar Bayti), Lafofa, jellaba, fellata, Nuer, Dinka, Shilluk
Dembalo	Hawazma/Halafa (El Togia), Liri Nuba
Dallas	Hawazma/Halafa (El Togia), Liri Nuba
Tomria	Hawazma/Halafa (Awlad Ghonaym)
Lokolak	Hawazma/Halafa (Awlad Ghonaym), Kawahla/Bederin
Tiro	Kawahla
Romala	Lafofa Nuba
al Khor	Lafofa, jellaba, fellata/Muwalid
Debbe	Lafofa Nuba
Tokoi	Lafofa Nuba
Tela	Lafofa Nuba
Um Shatta	Kawahla/Bederin, Lafofa Nuba
Sjek	Talasa

Pastoral groups with seasonal presence in the area:

Hawazma: Abd el-Ali (Dar Bayti, Awlad Ghabosh), Rawauga, Habbania, *fellata* Umbororo: the Woyla section

Kordofan. The sandy areas, as well as the availability of water along the mountain, are of course important factors in explaining the settlement patterns. The annual rainfall is between 700 and 800 mm, making a stable adaptation to crop farming possible. This is also the most important economic activity. People cultivate sorghum, Pennisetum and beans as staple crops, in addition to cash crops, like groundnuts and cotton. They cultivate them on different types of fields called "house fields" "near fields" and "far fields". The first two are in or around the villages on the sandy soil. Varieties of sorghum, maize and beans that ripen rapidly, are planted here, together with peanuts. For the majority of people, however, the far fields are the most important economically. They are located away from the mountain, on the clay plains and are planted with slow ripening sorghum in June and harvested in January and February. Apart from rain fed cultivation, people keep some animals. Cattle, goats, and some sheep and camels are the most common.

In addition to small-holder cultivation, the region also presents us with

Map 2.　　*Sketch-map of Liri villages*

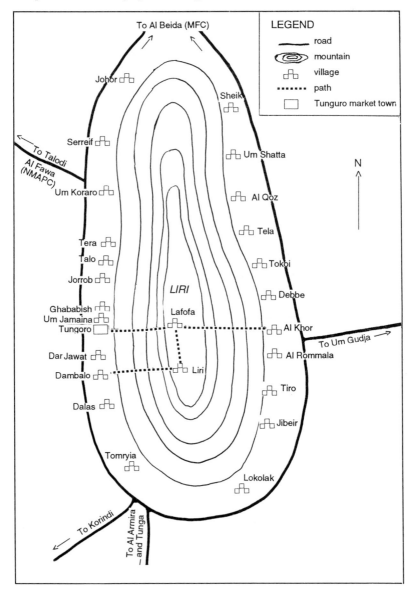

some agricultural schemes that have been introduced as a result of public development policies. One type is the mechanized small-holder scheme administered by the Nuba Mountains Agricultural Production Corporation (NMAPC). Farmers are supposed to grow cotton and sorghum in ro-

Map 3. *Sketch-map of Tunguro*

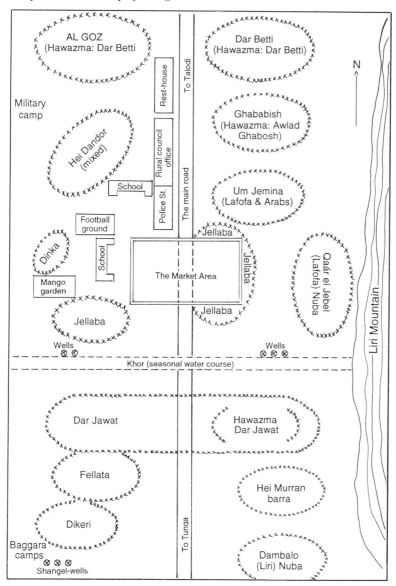

tation, hiring mechanical equipment from NMAPC. There are four schemes of this type in the Southern Nuba Mountain region: Gardud, Taboli, Um Dual and Al Fawa. Of these, Al Fawa is closest to Liri and the most important for the people of Liri.

Figure 1.   *Idealized farming organization in Liri*

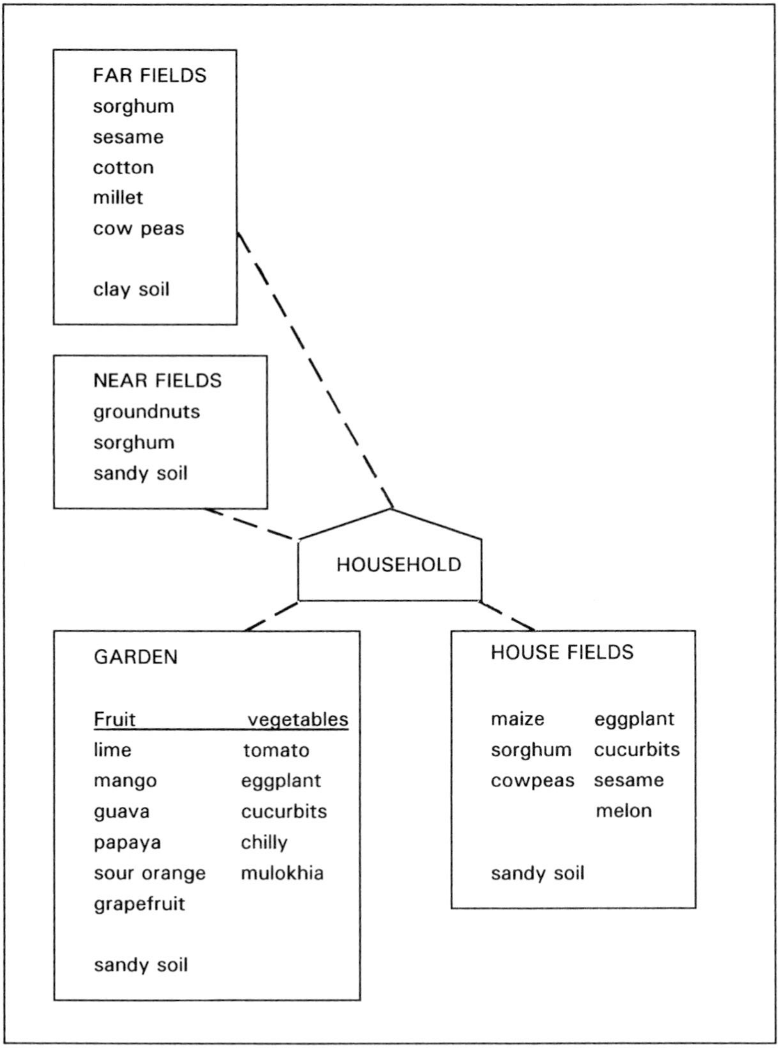

```
┌─────────────────────────────────────────────────────────────────┐
│  ┌─────────────────────┐                                         │
│  │ FAR FIELDS          │                                         │
│  │ sorghum             │                                         │
│  │ sesame              │                                         │
│  │ cotton              │                                         │
│  │ millet              │                                         │
│  │ cow peas            │                                         │
│  │                     │                                         │
│  │ clay soil           │                                         │
│  └─────────────────────┘                                         │
│  ┌─────────────────────┐                                         │
│  │ NEAR FIELDS         │                                         │
│  │ groundnuts          │                                         │
│  │ sorghum             │                                         │
│  │ sandy soil          │                                         │
│  └─────────────────────┘                                         │
│                          ┌──────────────┐                        │
│                          │  HOUSEHOLD   │                        │
│                          └──────────────┘                        │
│  ┌─────────────────────┐         ┌─────────────────────┐         │
│  │ GARDEN              │         │ HOUSE FIELDS        │         │
│  │ Fruit    vegetables │         │ maize    eggplant   │         │
│  │ lime     tomato     │         │ sorghum  cucurbits  │         │
│  │ mango    eggplant   │         │ cowpeas  sesame     │         │
│  │ guava    cucurbits  │         │          melon      │         │
│  │ papaya   chilly     │         │                     │         │
│  │ sour orange mulokhia│         │ sandy soil          │         │
│  │ grapefruit          │         └─────────────────────┘         │
│  │ sandy soil          │                                         │
│  └─────────────────────┘                                         │
└─────────────────────────────────────────────────────────────────┘
```

Adapted from Hunting Technical Services, 1980.

The second type of scheme is the large mechanized farm for the cultivation of sorghum. There are two such schemes, administered by the Mechanized Farming Corporation, made up of farms of 1,000 *feddan* (about 1,000 acres) each. Al Beida is the larger scheme and Tusi the smaller.

Apart from the settled cultivators, there are groups of nomadic pastoralists who are present during certain parts of the year. They are Bag-

Map 4. *Agricultural schemes in the southern part of Rashad*

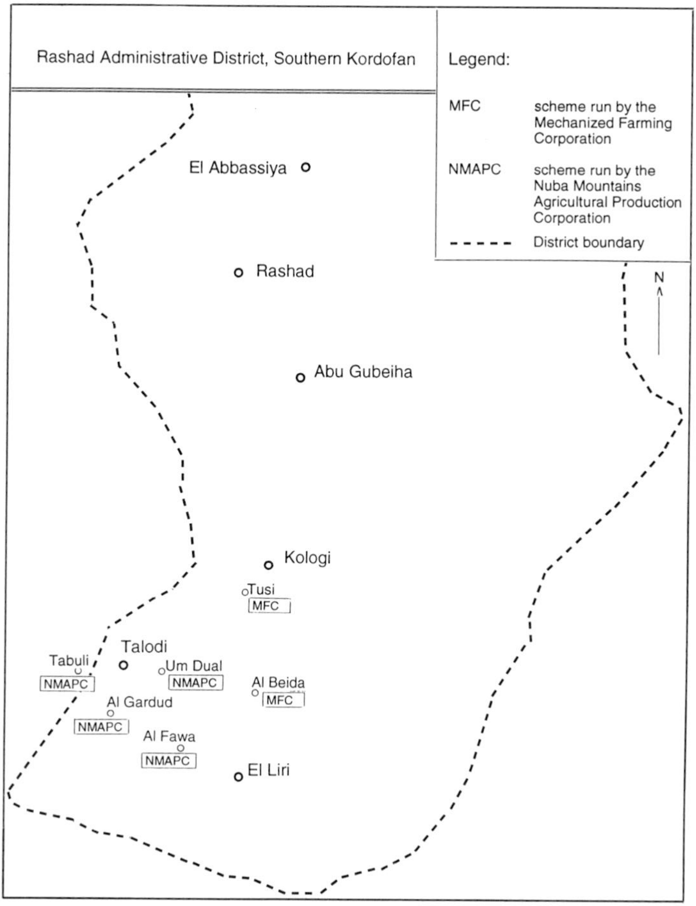

gara Arabs (primarily Hawazma) and some nomadic West African groups (Fulanis in the Sudan are called *fellata Umbororo*). These groups move over long distances, spending the rainy season on the sandy areas of Northern Kordofan Province, moving southwards into the Nuba Mountains as the dry season starts and staying there, with trips into Upper Nile Province for dry season grazing. For the southern Nuba Mountains, then, pastoralist camps are part of the dry season pattern.

The administrative district

Administratively this area makes up the southern end of the Rashad administrative district, the former Tegali District which takes its name from the old, pre-colonial Tegali kingdom. Liri is part of the Talodi Rural

Council and in Liri itself there is a small office with an RC-clerk. The Talodi Council oversees the activities of four crop markets, two of which are in Liri; three slaughter markets, one in Liri; three water pumps, one in Liri, eight *"hafir"* (basins for collecting rain water); one hospital with a medical doctor (in Talodi); three health stations, two in Liri with nurses; three police stations, one in Liri; three post offices, one i Liri; three secondary schools, two for boys, one for girls (all in Talodi); 12 elementary schools, of which three are in Liri (two for boys and one for girls), and two cotton ginneries.

SETTLEMENT PROCESSES

One major characteristic of this region is that it is inhabited by many groups that are not original inhabitants of the area. The only people who might be said to be indigeneous to Liri are the Liri Nuba. For the rest, their migrations to Liri are related to various developments in nineteenth and twentieth century Sudan. We said in the General Introduction that the Talasa Nuba is probably a branch of the Korongo which came to Liri around 1825–30, following a drought in the Tabuli area (Stevenson, 1984). The Lafofa came as a result of the unrest in the southern Nuba Mountains during the Mahdia, i.e. the late 1880s. The Hawazma and Kawahla Arabs also came during this period of major unrest.

The other groups have come in different "waves" of immigration related to different historical conditions during this century. The most important group to settle in Liri after 1900 was the *jellaba* group of traders. They were seeking the benefits of new opportunities offered by commercialization, e.g. trade in consumer goods, agricultural products, animals, and spare parts. Their settlement dates back to the 1920s and 1930s. The people called *fellata* have come in two waves. Firstly, in the period around 1920, when many West Africans were traversing the Sudan, they settled in different places. Secondly, in the 1970s, when the *jellaba* in Liri left the consumer trade for mechanized schemes. This opened up a new niche in the Liri market and new *fellata* migrants moved in to take over. Finally, the Southerners have come either individually as servants of the *jellaba*, or in groups during the 1970s, mainly as agricultural labourers on the *jellaba* schemes.

Escaping unrest: Lafofa, Hawazma and Kawahla

The arrival of the Lafofa, Hawazma and Kawahla groups is related to the situation on the southern frontier in eighteenth and nineteenth century Sudan. The distribution of adaptive groups in the region during this period was very much influenced by the problem of security. The Nuba Mountain Range was a frontier region, like the Ingessana and Dar Fartit,

(James, 1977; Spaulding, 1980; O'Fahey, 1982), being subject to human and economic exploitation by the various powerholders that controlled the regions to the north. These powerholders were, first, the pre-colonial savanna states, Funj and Darfur, the Turco-Egyptian regime (after 1821) and finally the Mahdist state (Hill, 1959; Holt, 1970; O'Fahey, 1980; Spaulding, 1985). For our area it is significant that it was within the area of one of the smaller pre-colonial states, the Tegali kingdom (Elles, 1935; Ewald, 1982). The general theme during this period was the exploitation of the Nuba Mountains for ivory, gold and, most importantly, slaves. All the powerholders mentioned were Muslims, who were attacking the non-Muslim Nuba populations; the Nuba being the main target of slave raids. A basic problem for the Nuba was thus how to organize their defence, in order to survive in their home areas.

The identity of the slave hunters varied, but apart from official slave hunting expeditions organized by the states themselves, the main groups involved were the immigrant groups, i.e. the Hawazma pastoralists and the *jellaba* traders. The Hawazma used the Nuba Mountains area for pasture, which brought them deep into the mountains and into contact with the inhabitants. During these migrations the Hawazma would raid and enslave different Nuba groups. The system varied. In some hills they would develop relations with Nuba leaders, who would provide slaves from other groups in order to save their own populations. In other areas the Nuba were raided directly by the pastoralists. In all instances, however, the system was based on physical superiority.

For the pastoralists, the slaves served many purposes. They were used as herders as well as cultivators on the fields the pastoralists had in the northern parts of the mountains, where they had their bases. Slaves were also passed on to the rulers of the Northern Sudan as payment for taxes that otherwise would have been paid in animals. The institution of slavery and the pastoralists' involvement in slave raids solved a number of problems within the pastoral adaptation, like labour problems as well as problems with the rulers. It also left the pastoralists with the time to supplement their incomes by hunting ostriches, giraffes and elephants, which were all important in the trade of the day.

The traders' involvement in slave catching and the slave trade was also significant. They organized slave raiding parties, called *ghazwa* and *kubbaniyya* (O'Fahey, 1985) and went into the mountains to hunt for Nuba. Many traders became rich through these activities and the capital gained through the slave trade became the start of many *jellaba* trading houses in the west.

The basic pattern of this exploitation of the Nuba Mountains did not change much throughout the period before 1900, except for in the intensity of exploitation. The Turco-Egyptian regime demanded more slaves and taxes from the inhabitants than had the pre-colonial kingdoms, and they had a stronger military machine for securing what they wanted. The level of exploitation thus increased in the nineteenth century (Ewald, 1982; Mercer, 1971). But generally, developments during these periods left the Arab pastoralists and the traders as superior groups, able to exploit the Nuba inhabitants. The two groups were involved in mutual relations that benefited them both. The traders used pastoralists as slave hunters and also traded with them. The traveller Petherick noted an interesting example

> The Turks used to capture cattle from the Baggara in Southern Kordofan as a kind of tribute, but as the shipments to Egypt came to an end, the Turks converted some of the cattle into cash by selling them to local jellaba. The latter brought the animals back to the Baggara and bartered them for slaves and ivory, valuable commodities in the jellaba traffic. (Petherick 1861:321)

For the Nuba a basic problem was how to organize themselves for defence in order to survive in their home areas. This could partly be done by hiding in their mountains where the horses of the slave raiders could not enter, the task of defence therefore being made easier. But political allegiances were also at work, showing that the situation was not completely anarchic.

Within Tegale there were smaller political units ruled over by local leaders called *Meks*. They owed allegiance to greater rulers above them, and the link was maintained through payments of tribute. This description is particularly relevant for the Lafofa who, before settling in Liri, lived in Tikeim, an area to the east of the Liri mountain. Tikeim was part of the area controlled by one of the Tegale *Meks*, at *Jebel* Gedir (Elles, 1935). The *Mek* of Gedir ruled over areas of Nuba inhabitants as well as various Arab groups. The people under him were the Kau, Fungor, Werni, Kalogi, Tira, Talodi and possibly eastern Moro (Elles, 1935:15). My own material shows that according to the Lafofa tradition a daughter of the Lafofa *Mek*, Deldung, was married to the *Mek* Bosh of Gedir, indicating the existence of a political relationship which could well be related to the need for security (see Spaulding, 1980 and Ewald, 1982 and 1988 for a discussion).

Although the pattern of general exploitation of the Nuba Mountains did not change much throughout the time before 1900, developments during the Mahdia period increased the pressure on these outlying areas and led to the dramatic resettlement of various groups. The most important of these developments was the outbreak of war in the 1880s. First, the Tegali rulers refused to join the Mahdi and were severely punished for this during the reign of the *Khalifa* Abdullahi. Troops were sent under the leadership of Hamdan Abu Anga and El Nur 'Angara to punish Tegale (1886–87). Abu Anga penetrated as far south as *Jebel* Gedir where he defeated the local *Mek* Bosh.

One effect of this was a general flight of people towards the south and a relocation of people into new areas. Thus Vicars-Miles, a later British administrator, noted in one report: "During the Mahdia the people of Gedir were repeatedly attacked and overcome. Many of their Nuba supporters were captured and killed, and most of the remainder fled to Talodi and Liri" (Vicars-Miles, 1934). Or, in the more dramatic words of R.J. Elles, "Abu Anja penetrated as far south as Gedir, where he defeated *Mek* Bosh with great slaughter; men and baboons together fled southwards towards Murnung" (Elles, 1935:26).

Judging from figures, unreliable though they probably are, there was every reason to escape. Figures show that from a pre-Mahdia population in Kordofan province of 1,800,000 the number of inhabitants fell to 550,000 in 1903. 600,000 died of disease while 650,000 are estimated to have perished because of warfare (McLoughlin, 1962:387). Because of these upheavals, several groups living in the southern Nuba Mountains date their arrival at their present habitats to that period. This also holds for the Lafofa migration to Liri.

Another group that was also affected was the pastoral Hawazma. During the Mahdia, the *Khalifa* demanded that the Baggara should come to Omdurman. Some groups obeyed, others did not. The Hawazma in our region were among the latter and went into hiding in the mountains. This brought about the development of new relations between the Hawazma and the Nuba. Due to Hawazma dependence on the assistance of locgl populations to help them escape Mahdist troops, there developed more peaceful relationships than before, now with some cases of intermarriage between Nuba and Arabs (Abdel Hamid Mohamed Osman, 1986). These developments also have led some Hawazma to Liri, to settle together with people they had earlier hunted for slaves.

One important point about the people in Liri who today claim *Hawazma* descent is that many of them are not of "pure" Arab ancestry. They are the descendants of former slaves who have taken on the tribal identity of their former masters. As we saw, the nomadic groups that came into the area of the Tegale kingdom around the middle of the eighteenth century were allowed to make slave raids on certain hills. To pay their allegiance to the kings of Tegale the nomads probably gave some of these slaves to him. The rest were used as herders, and also as cultivators in the areas where the nomads were cultivating. For the Hawazma, Awlad Abd el Ali, this meant the Dilling area, where they had rain fed cultivation on the sandy soil. Having their *dar* (home area) that far north in the Nuba Mountains also meant that they were rather close to the territories that were under the direct control of the big powers of

Funj and Darfur, and they might also have had to pay taxes to them. Rather than pay in cattle they might make this payment in slaves, meaning that part of the slave population was used for that purpose, probably ending up as soldiers in the slave armies (*jihadiyya*). Such armies made up of slave soldiers were also common under Turkish rule and the custom was later to be taken over by the Mahdist rulers. With the wars and general unrest during the Mahdia, many of these slave soldiers managed to run away. Liri, being at the periphery of events, can easily be seen as an attractive place for people who were running away. Old informants mentioned Tira, Heiban and Nyimang as the home areas of the ancestors of some of the people who today claim Hawazma descent.

The *Kawahla* settlement in Liri is also related to events in the area of the *Mek* of Gedir. In a historical note on the Kawahla, Captain Vicars-Miles describes how a feud between two Kawahla *khasm-baits*, the Halaifi and the Bederin, led them to approach the *Mek* of Gedir to have him settle the dispute. They thus came under his rule at the beginning of the Mahdia. And as the Nuba the Kawahla fled during the troubles that haunted the area. Thus Vicars-Miles noted

> During the Mahdia the people of Gedir were repeatedly attacked and overcome. Many of their Nuba supporters were captured or killed and most of the reminder fled to Talodi and El Liri. The Kawahla also did not join the Mahdi. There followed a period of continued raids and many of the Kawahla fled to El Liri while others joined the Lukha Nuba who seem to have defended themselves to some purpose. (Vicars-Miles, 1934)

Towards the end of the nineteenth century, then, the settlement pattern in Liri was characterized by a Nuba population (including the Liri and the Talasa) living up in the mountain and having most of its cultivation there. The people who claimed Hawazma descent were living on the plain on the western side, and the Kawahla on the eastern side of the mountain. There was not the structure of villages along the mountain that we see today. People were clustered according to social links, mostly for defence purposes. The slave trade was also going on, and there was a small center on the eastern side of the mountain where such trade was carried out. The relationship between the Hawazma and the Kawahla was hostile and tribal fights went on.

Seeking opportunities: Jellaba, Fellata, Southerners

The most important group to settle in Liri in this century is the *jellaba* group of traders. Members of the jellaba groups in the Sudan, who are of Arab and Nubian origin, have spread throughout the Sudan, from the Nile Valley, exploiting different possibilities and founding different communities on their way. In the earlier centuries they dealt in slaves, gum arabic, ivory, salt and other goods that were transported in the caravans that traversed the Sudan. In this century, trade in consumer goods, agricultural products, animals and spare parts has taken over as economically the most significant. Lorries were brought in to improve transport; investments were made in urban housing, in wage labour for cash crop production, in labour and technology for mechanized farming, in the auxiliary services and eventually in industrial enterprises. During all this time the development of *jellaba* businesses has been characterized by entrepreneurial activity and the exploitation of new possibilities as they arose within the political and economic environment (Manger, ed., 1984).

The *jellaba* started arriving in Liri early this century. This coincided with the early British attempts at integrating and developing the southern Nuba Mountains. Compared to the earlier period, the years of the British rule in the Nuba Mountains brought profound changes. Two such changes were the pacification of the area and the abolition of slavery. The British strategy, finding the Nuba in their hills and the Arabs on the plains, was first to bring the Arabs under control. They posed the most serious military threat but were also of immediate economic interest to the British, since they had cattle, the only cash commodity of the day. After the Arabs had been pacified, the Nuba were brought under control, often through punitive patrols and forced down-migration from their hills into the plains, where they could be more easily controlled (Huddleston, 1947; Vicars-Miles, 1934).

The British presence also brought changes to the economic environment of the area. To rule the region the British established military and administrative towns, centres which also grew into markets where the expanding exchange of goods could take place. Talodi, Kalogi and Liri were all such market-places. Contact between these towns and others was improved by the construction of new roads and the introduction of motorized vehicles. Developments thus moved towards opening up the earlier closed area. But this was counteracted by another element of British policy, which was to keep the Nuba apart from the Arab populations to avoid processes of Arabization and Islamization. The main tool to achieve this was the introduction of the Closed District Ordinance in 1922. This ordinance restricted and regulated travels in Darfur, Bahr el-Ghazal, Mongalla, and most of the Nuba Mountains and Upper Nile Provinces (Daly, 1980). The aims of British policies in the area thus appear to be contradictory, and they led to several changes in strategies for developing the area (Nasr, 1971).

The early traders in Liri came from the area just south of Khartoum. From their home areas they moved south to Malakal, and from there some of them continued northwards again until they reached Liri. This was at the turn of the century, and none of the persons involved are left, nor are their descendants any longer directly involved in trade. A second "wave" of traders came to the area a bit later and they are the ones who have dominated trade in Liri until today. Of those concerning us here, some came from Omdurman, others from Ed Dueim, and Kawa along the White Nile. Later on people from Shireq along the Blue Nile, as well as from Kosti and El Obeid, came to settle. They all participated in trade, as well as in the cultivation of cash crops (cotton and peanuts). This wave of newcomers is related to the lifting of the "Closed District Ordinance" in 1937.

The two *jellaba* communities in Liri are Tunguru and al Khor. In Tunguru there are traders from Omdurman, Ed Dueim, Kawa, Shireq, Rufa'a, Kosti and El Obeid. In al Khor a majority of traders come from Um Jer, a village near Ed Dueim.

Another group that is now moving into Liri, primarily because of possibilities within the commercial sector, are members of the *fellata* group. They came to fill in the empty space in the consumer goods market that is left by the *jellaba* shift from trade to mechanized farming. These developments started in the early 1970s, when the Liri *jellaba* started investing in tractors and discers (the first came in 1971) and expanded their cultivated areas considerably. From 1976, al Beida was made into a Mechanized Farming Scheme with individual schemes of 1,000 *feddan* (1,040 acres) being allocated to people who could raise the necessary capital. With the involvement of the *jellaba* traders in this new sector, the consumer goods trade was left as an open niche in Liri and many of the *fellata* came to take up these opportunities. The migration is fairly similar in nature to that of the *jellaba*. A single person comes first and later brings his family. The Liri *fellata*, who are now moving in, come from Abu Gibeha in the Nuba Mountains, while others come from Khartoum. In Liri they all live in the market center of Tunguru.

The settlement of *fellata* in Liri is, however, of older origin and relates to the migrations of West Africans throughout the Sudan early this century. *fellata* settlements in the Nuba Mountains probably date back to the pre-Mahdia period (Hassoun 1952:76). It was, however, with the introduction of cotton cultivation that the main settlement began, and the people, who claim *fellata muwallid* and *Takarir* descent, settled in some Liri villages (particularly al Khor and Talo) in the early 1920s (see e.g. Hassoun, op.cit.; Warburg, 1971; Duffield, 1981). The term "*muwallid*" is Arabic for "born in the Sudan" and "*Takarir*" is a generic term used for black Muslims coming from Nigeria and the Chad Basin, in this case Wadai and Darfur. It was also during this period that the term "*fellata*" started to be used for *all* West African groups.

The Southerners who now live in Liri have come there mainly as household servants of the *jellaba* community and as agricultural labourers on the fields of the traders. The number rose rapidly through the 1970s, when the mechanized farming schemes were introduced, greatly increasing the need for labour power. In the 1980s the civil war lead to another influx of people from the south. The groups represented are Nuer, Dinka and Shilluk, who have their own quarters in Tunguru. Some of them stay in Liri throughout the year, making ends meet by working as water carriers and doing other types of daily wage work, again primarily for the *jellaba*.

Seeking pasture: Hawazma and Fellata Umbororo

The British policies of pacification and economic development also affected the pastoral Hawazma. For the pastoralists, the abolition of slavery took away their main supply of labour and forced them to start doing the herding and cultivating themselves. Many pastoralists lost much of their livestock during the Mahdist wars and were therefore less nomadic than before. They took up cultivation in the Nuba Mountains, especially cotton growing, to earn money to rebuild their herds. This led many of the Hawazma into an agro-pastoral adaptation, and only a minority continued to lead a purely pastoral life. There thus developed a division of labour among the Hawazma in which some members of a family would be nomadic, while others would be sedentary and exploit local opportunities. Similarly, with the growth of the urban centres, new markets developed for milk and members of the pastoralist groups also settled here, keeping milch cows in town and selling milk to the inhabitants. Finally, wage labour within the towns provided a new opportunity that was seized upon (Osman, 1984). In Liri such links between settled Hawazma and pastoral Hawazma also developed.

ESTABLISHING ADMINISTRATIVE STRUCTURES

An important development during this century is the establishment of effective local and regional administrations throughout the Nuba Mountains. In our area this started with the British policy of rebuilding the administrative structure of the eastern and southern *jebels*. This policy also built upon the structure that was already there and was represented by the Tegale Kingdom. The British found the kingdom disintegrated, with isolated groups of people defending themselves from their hills. Within its borders the kingdom contained Baggara Arabs, Arabized Nuba, ex-slave settlements, settled westerners and purely pagan groups. The problems the British faced were manifold. First they had to pacify the Nuba area. Thus, Huddleston, in his foreword to Nadel's book on the Nuba wrote

> In the early days, the contact of the administration with the Nuba had fre-
> quently culminated in a small military patrol directed now against one hill
> and now against another. (Nadel, 1947:xi)

A punitive patrol was sent to Liri as late as 1929 (the Lafofa expedition),
but on the whole the 1920s represent the start of a more coherent British
policy in the Nuba Mountains. In the field of administration, the most important part of the policy was to restore the disintegrated fragments of
the old Tegale "empire" and turn it into a Rural District Council on the
basis of the model of Native Administration. This was, as we know, a policy that aimed at installing tribal leaders in positions of *nazirs* and *omdas*
(*mek*, term used for Nuba leaders) and giving them the power to pass
judgement on conflicts as well as to collect taxes.

For Tegale, the first moves were made in the northern areas, especially
important being the moving of the capital from Kirain to Abbasiya, and
the opening of a new road between Rashad and Abbasiya in 1925. The
southern area was integrated later, step by step. First, the Awlad Himeid
nazir, Radi Kambal, agreed to act as a *wakil* of the Tegale *mek* in the south
and thus brought his tribe and area under the Tegale administration. As
part of the settlement, this move brought in not only the Awlad Himeid
but also the Kenana and Kawahla of Kalogi, thus opening up for the joining of Liri and Talodi.

The British also put great emphasis on building a court system that
would help in this administration of people. They accepted customary
ways of doing it, for instance, courts could be organized on a tribal basis
with the *nazir* as the head judge. They also accepted the Islamic part of
customary law and let a Muslim *faqi* act as "*alim*" at the *nazir*'s courts. He
was supposed to deal with cases of personal law, marriages, divorce etc.

This system was not extended to the Nuba. They were given their own
customary courts in which the *meks* could judge, with the aid of the *kujor*
etc. As the power of these people was broken, judging cases increasingly
became a matter for British inspectors. Today the Nuba are within the
judicial system of the Sudan.

Appointing a nazir in Liri

This process was finalized in Liri in 1937 (Kalogi in the early 1920s, while
Talodi joined in 1945). The developments in Liri were also characterized
by tribal quarrels over leadership but on one issue they joined forces: that
of rejecting the British wish to join Liri to the Kalogi Kawahla.

In the internal struggle for leadership, the Kawahla did not succeed
and it became an internal competition between a leader from the Dar
Betti of the Awlad Abd el Ali and one from the Halafa. The British accepted the Halafa candidate as *nazir*, and he acted from about 1900 until
his death in 1927. After his death the British gave the *nazirate* to a man

Figure 2. *Tribal administrative positions in the Sudan until 1972*

from Awlad Abd el Ali/Awlad Ghabosh, but this appointment did not turn out satisfactorily and the British decided to bring in an outsider. The people from Liri were given a choice of three persons, all of whom held posts in the police. The forum that selected the *nazir* was the group of local *omdas* and *sheikhs*, and they eventually accepted Sherif Osman from Kordofan as their *nazir*. The British motive for choosing an outsider is indicated by the following entry in an administrative protocol from Kalogi, made by Ellis at about the same time: "The Kawahla here and at El Liri seem to have been allowed to dodge about how they like, and the result is fairly complete chaos."

And the troubles were to continue under the new *nazir*. As one of his early acts as *nazir*, Sherif Osman appointed a new *omda* over the Kawahla, replacing one who had opposed his nomination. During this new *omda*-ship, the conflicts between the Kawahla and the Hawazma gained new momentum as the new *omda* started to mobilize support from his own people as well as from the Nuba against the Hawazma, whom he called "former slaves" (*abid*) as opposed to the Kawahla/Nuba who were freeborn (*hurr*). The issue was the control of land. In this strategy he had the support of the Lafofa *mek*, Kobango.

In this context, a major conflict developed between the *nazir* Sherif and Kobango, who was ensconced in his mountain village. The issue was the payment of poll tax, and the situation developed to a point where the British sent in a punitive patrol, supported by aircraft that bombed the village. Kobango was sent to the Kober jail in Khartoum together with some of his tribesmen, where he died.

Kobango's action was related to the wider problems in Liri; and after having done away with the Nuba the British officers, Oakley and Bell, travelled around to all *omdas* and *sheikhs* to see if they supported the

Kawahla *omda* who was thought to be behind the troubles. The *omda*, it turned out, had little support and he was removed and sentenced to one year's imprisonment. Sherif Osman acted as *nazir* until 1938. The joining of Liri to the Tegale administration was, therefore, also completed during his period as leader.

In 1938, the son of the first Liri *nazir* from the Halafa was appointed *nazir*. He had been assistant (*wakil*) to Sherif Osman since 1934. His selection was partly because he was the son of the former *nazir*, but it also signified the importance of education as a criterion in the British selection of tribal leaders. In the mid-1920s the first primary school had been opened in Liri with three pupils, one of whom was to become the new *nazir*. The Liri school was closed after some years, but the three students were sent to Talodi to further their education. They all ended up in the medical services, the future *nazir* working at the local health station in Liri. He acted as *nazir* from 1938 until 1958 when the *nazirate* was taken away from the Halafa and given to the Kawahla.

The new Kawahla *nazir* was the grandson of the *omda* who had conspired together with the Lafofa. He also worked in the medical services as a medical assistant. He acted as *nazir* until the revolution of Nimeiri in May 1968, when this administrative system was formally abolished.

This overview shows how things slowly settled down in Liri and how the tribal leadership positions and the appointments to such posts also tell the story about group relationships in Liri. The first *nazir* became a leader on the basis of his position of strength, whereas the later ones were appointed by the British who wanted to strike a balance between the need for continuity of leadership and the need for literate people who could act as tax collectors and judges, write reports, etc.

The "slave–freeman" distinction in contemporary politics

As we saw above, a conflict developed around the use of terms like slave (*abid*) and freeman (*hurr*) and this usage had implications for political alliances and political action. A Kawahla leader could mobilize the Lafofa against the Hawazma, by referring to their past as run-away slaves. This distinction did not disappear with the events of the 1930s. In 1984, when a new *nazir* was to be elected, the same issues were debated and created controversy.

With the Nimeiri regime's policy of decentralization in the early 1980s, through which new provincial units were given extended powers, some of the regional governors, notably the ones in Kordofan and Darfur, decided to bring back the old Native Administration leadership model, and to give the tribal leaders back their old powers. As a result, *nazirs* were reinstated in 1984, among whom we find the Liri *nazir*.

This development signifies a major change in public policies towards local government in the Sudan, and dramatically shows the failure of the Nimeiri system and the problems faced by local government officers in carrying out their duties. During the years of the Nimeiri regime it became increasingly clear that its officers were not given the necessary respect and support of local populations. They were, therefore, inefficient in bringing in taxes, in catching criminals, and in solving other types of conflicts within local communities. Hence a reorganization was needed and the regional governors opted for the old tribal leadership model.

Given this background to the bringing back of the old leaders, one might believe that such a step-back by the authorities would be a popular move. But this was not the case in Liri. The fact is that the reinstatement of the Liri *nazir* was not an unproblematic act. The person in question was not wanted by a majority of the people, and his candidacy, therefore, provoked disputes among different groups in Liri. It was only through a direct appointment made by the District Commissioner of South Kordofan, that the post was secured for this particular person.

As I tried to follow the disputes and the discussions, it became evident that people were opposed to this man because of his handling of cases involving tribal interests during his earlier period in office, but it was also argued that he was unfit because he provoked old tribal conflicts in Liri. The most serious charge was that the *nazir* was stirring old sentiments about the former slave status of many groups in Liri, and that he had been using the slave-freeman (*abid– hurr*) identities as a basis on which to draw political support. The *nazir* claims he belongs to a line of freemen, and tried to mobilize support from others against those whom he claimed were of slave origin.

These discussions came as a surprise to me and thus I began the collection of the information that forms the basis of this section. The fact that many groups in Liri were of slave origin was not new to me; but as it did not appear to be at all relevant during my previous field-work, I was taken by surprise by the heated debates.

THE NUBA–ARAB DISTINCTION

Apart from pacifying the Nuba area, British policies towards the Nuba Mountains were dominated by their wish and determination to keep the Nuba apart from the Arabic population and to promote development for the Nuba without turning them into Arabized Muslims. This policy has been documented in various fields (see e.g. Sanderson, 1963 and Nasr, 1971). Small entries in government reports also indicate that the administrators were well aware of this overall strategy. For instance, in February 1933 Mr. Hawkesworth was said to have told the Nuba at Werni to stick to their tribal customs. In an entry, about a dispute settlement between the Kawahla tribe and the Tira Nuba, one important point noted is that visiting between the two tribes should be constrained, as it leads to Arabization, which must at all costs be avoided. It is also noted that the administrators must find ways to prevent the Arabization of the Nuba without making them hostile to the Arabs.

Educating the Nuba

The British views on socio-cultural integration between the Nuba and Arabs come out clearly in the field of *education*. The policies of education show how the administrators experimented with different types of schools and different languages of instruction as well as with involvement by Christian missionaries, all in order to contain the Nuba as an indigenous group, which differed from the Arabized Muslim population.

The policy of education was dependent on who at any particular time was governor of Kordofan and the systems in the Nuba Mountains were shaped during the times of Gillan and Newbold. Gillan tried to teach Arabic to the Nuba in Roman script, to block the immediate relation between the Arabic language and Islamic religion. When Newbold took over in 1932, however, he saw that the Nuba would need Arabic in Arabic letters in order to get jobs, and that it would also help improve contact between Arab and Nuba chiefs. He thus opened the way for the teaching of Arabic to Nuba people in Arabic script. In 1940 the British abandoned the special schools for Nuba children and as of this date they could attend any school. The importance of education to the Nuba was not so much for their intellectual enlightenment, as to produce people capable of working for the government, e.g. clerks for the *Meks*, staff for the police, army, medical services, agriculture, ginneries as well as clerks. The appointment of the third *nazir* of Liri, as described earlier, is a case in point.

Britsh policies also show regional differences. Those areas with an Arab population or a population of Nuba stock that had long been Islamized were treated as "Northern" and offered their education in Arabic, and the Koranic schools, *khalwas*, were allowed to operate. This applied to the Tegale areas and hence also to the Liri region. The Central Nuba areas were treated differently. Here the Government experimented with Christian mission education and also with secular education in *kuttab* schools (Sanderson, 1963; A.A.R. Nasr, 1971).

The Role of Islam

Although the British in the eastern areas (Tegale) to some extent accepted the existence of Islamic influence and allowed Islamic forces to work, this did not occur without problems arising. These problems were related to the British fear of Islam as a political force following the Mahdia period.

The period after the fall of the Mahdi was one of religious unrest in the Sudan, an unrest that also led to incidents in the Nuba Mountains. The problem as viewed by the British was that of *sufism*. The British adminis-tration under Wingate developed a policy of support and encourage-ment to orthodox Islam, creating a Board of *Ulema* in 1901, building mosques, appointing judges (*qadis*) to judge according to *sharia* law, etc. (Warburg, 1971:96).

The Islamic brotherhoods, however, were restricted and regarded as a form of dangerous fanatism that could create political problems. It is a fact that in the early years of the new century hardly a year passed with-out some religious uprising or some *fuqara* (sing. *faqi*, pl. *fuqara*) being ar-rested and deported. Death penalties were not uncommon after such up-risings (see Warberg, op.cit.:100ff.). The uprisings usually started when a local *faqi* declared himself a new *mahdi* or as *nebbi Isa* (the prophet Jesus), secured some supporters, and attacked a British station. The most im-portant uprising under Wingate took place in 1908, when Abd el-Gadir Muhammed Imam Wad Habuba and his followers attacked and killed some British administrators in the Masalamiya district of the Blue Nile Province.

The uprisings that took place in the Nuba Mountains are of a later date. The British thought first that the 1906 Talodi Mutiny had religious overtones, but it turned out to be related to the Government's policies on slave raiding. However, in 1912 there was an uprising in the Eastern *jebels*, started by a Tunisian *faqi*. He proclaimed himself *mahdi* near *jebel* Gedir but was shot dead with seven of his followers by the British. This "*sherifi* uprising" as it is called was the first of several incidents.

In 1915 a *fellata faqi*, Ahmed Omer, proclaimed himself *nebbi* Isa and retreated to *jebel* Gedir. This case is interesting because it was the first time a West African (*fellata*) was involved in such an event. The British had been positive to the *fellata* and their contribution to the economy, but in 1910 it was clear that their numbers were increasing fast and that they represented a potential threat. For example, after the battle of Burmi in 1903, some 25,000 Fulani refugees fled from Nigeria and settled in the Sudan especially along the Blue Nile where the British gave them land. Ahmed Omer, who originally came from Sokoto in Nigeria, first settled in Omdurman but later went to the Nuba Mountains encouraging fellow *fellata* to follow him. Although his success was meager, some did follow him.

The end of this uprising started a period of peace in the Eastern dis-trict, but elsewhere in the Nuba Mountains the problems continued. A serious incident took place in 1915 in *jebel* Miri, close to Kadugli, in which a Nuba *mek*, Fiki Ali, rebelled. But this incident turned out to be a local af-fair. On the whole, the religious uprisings were small incidents; but since the Mahdia had happened only a decade before, the British were sensitive to religious unrest. This continued up until the 1920s. Although during WWI the British started to treat the *sufi* leadership with less hostility, a note in a report from Abu Gibeiha (June 1923) says

> Abba Island fever: no one representing himself as wakil of Abdel Rahman el Mahdi be allowed in without written permission. (A/R el Mahdi was the son of the Mahdi, born after his death. Abba Island is the center of the Ansar leadership).

Islamic missionaries

The above discussion gives an important context for our understanding of the developments in Liri. This is so because a significant Islamic influence was brought to Liri by a *fellata*. He did not present himself as a prophet, but did work within the structure of an Islamic brotherhood, a *tariqa*.

Such brotherhoods acted as an important factor through which the Lafofa and others were influenced and taught new values and norms. In Liri the *Qadiriyya* sect is the dominant one, and within this sect is the *Makashfiyya* branch with its center at Gezira. The history of this *tariqa* in the southern Nuba Mountains in general and in Liri in particular goes back to the beginning of the present century and is related to the coming in 1906 of a *faqi* (Islamic Holy Man) to work as a missionary. He was *sheikh* Bernawi, a West African, who had been initiated by the leader of the *tariqa*, the *Makashif*. He travelled around for many years, teaching the locals, as well as intermarrying with them. Eventually he settled down in Liri and built his *mesid* (local center) there. After his death his son, *sheikh* Abdel Bagi, took over as religious leader and is currently the religious leader in Liri.

Around these leaders a group of followers developed, the dervishes (*faqi/fuqara*). These local converts became propagators of the new religion among their own people. The *faqi* performs the Islamic rituals at important events like name-giving, circumcision, marriage and death. He also operates as a healer to the extent he has been given power (*baraka*) to do so.

The Qadiriyya in Liri appears as a ritual and organizational unit with the great *sheikh* at the pivotal point, and with lesser *sheikhs* as his representatives. This network of dervishes is very important for teaching illiterate people about Islam. The teaching of Muhamed and the content of the Koran are conveyed through direct contact between a *sheikh* and his followers. To an adherent, being a Muslim thus means going to the places where the teaching goes on, be it a *noba* dance, a *karama*, a wedding in the village or a visit to the *mesid*.

Islamization, Arabization and Sudanization

Developments such as those sketched above relate directly to the contemporary distribution of social power on the plural scene in Liri. We have seen how this distribution of power is clearly in favour of the Arabic groups against the non-Arabs and non-Muslims. This is related to the long history of Arabization and Islamization in the Sudan, through which local groups have adopted new cultural traits. There is also a contemporary process of change going on in the Sudan, which is not one of accepting the Islamic religion or Arabic language and customs alone, but rather that ethnically diverse groups living in the Sudanese periphery adapt to the dominant life-style of the centre. Non-Arab and non-Islamized groups like the Nuba show the most dramatic expression of such processes, but already Islamized Arab groups are also going through similar processes.

As we said in the General Introduction, this process does not mean that people only want to catch up with the mainstream Arabic culture, but rather that they want "materially and spiritually to participate as a member of the Sudanese top stratum of traders and officials, and to be taken seriously, be considered trust- and creditworthy throughout the Sudan" (Doornbos, 1984). This is a general process of social change in contemporary Sudan. Traders are among the major agents of this change, but so are modern schools, local courts and Islamic brotherhoods. This way of life is characterized by non-manual labour, non-drinking, seclusion of women, a clear public display of Islamic identity (Doornbos, op.cit.). In Liri, the *jellaba* represent such a way of life, while the Nuba represent the opposite. The Nuba are still considered a non-Muslim, non-Arab population, with a past history as slaves and they are still marginalized in society. Such a *stigma* on the Nuba identity is therefore an important point for understanding the Lafofa as they participate on the plural Liri scene.

RELATIONS IN THE ECONOMIC FIELD

An important arena of contact between the Nuba and the Arab population was in the economic field. In their early period in the Sudan the British built the Sennar Dam on the Blue Nile to get water for the Gezira irrigation project. To do this they needed many labourers, some of whom came from the Nuba Mountains. The people of the southern region, especially from Liri, were among the first to go (Vicars-Miles, 1934). But after some time, the British saw that this created "detribalized" Nuba. The migrants settled elsewhere in the country, took up Arab and Islamic customs, and showed several signs of cultural change, which the British wanted to avoid. Thus the Closed District Ordinance was introduced to regulate movements of people.

Another element was British awareness that, if they wanted the Nuba to stay at home, they had to create economic opportunities in their home areas. This, as well as the general need for revenue, led to the introduction in the early 1920s of the cultivation of cotton as a cash crop. The Nuba were already cultivating some cotton, short in staple and poor in quality, but one which suited their looms and required little work in the fields. The British attempted to introduce a higher quality cotton and the government scheme introducing new cotton in 1924 is generally considered to be the beginning of cotton growing in the Nuba Mountains. The first people to adopt it were the *jellaba*, followed by the pastoralists, whereas the Nuba were reluctant. But in the 1920s and 1930s there were large increases in the cultivation of cotton, and this success even made people leave grain production; thus endangering the food supply of the area. By the 1930s British administrators warned against food shortages and famine in bad years, and they encouraged people to grow some grain. They also began to introduce alternative food crops, such as groundnuts and sesame, that could also be used as cash crops (Vicars-Miles, ibid.).

The developments sketched above were to have an important impact on the various groups living in the region. For the pastoralists, the abolition of slavery took away their main labour supply and forced them to start herding and cultivating themselves. Many pastoralists had lost much of their livestock during the Mahdist wars and were, therefore, less nomadic than before. They took up cultivation in the Nuba Mountains, especially cotton growing, to earn money to rebuild their herds. This led many of the Hawazma into an agro-pastoral adaptation, and only a minority continued to lead a purely pastoral life.

For the Nuba, the most significant transition was their down-migration from the mountains into a safe life on the plains. This also meant a decrease in the intensive hill cultivation, as they transferred cultivation to the more fertile sand and clay plains. The Nuba, however, did not enter this economic development as early as the Arabs. Their past experiences made them reluctant to go into new activities, as did their limited cash needs. But eventually the Nuba also became integrated into the expanding economy of the area. They took on wage labour on the *jellaba* and Arab cotton farms, and started to cultivate the new crop themselves.

Through this process of economic development the *jellaba* managed to establish a central place for themselves in the economy of the region. Due to their capital and organizational experience (Manger, 1984), they were able to make a future for themselves, in spite of British reluctance and occasional active discouragement. The government was hostile to the *jellaba* because of their involvement in the slave trade and their gun-running to locals, and because it suspected them of cheating the Nuba and teaching them how to drink liquor. But from their bases in towns and market centres, the *jellaba* were an integral part of the regional economy, dominating trade as well as the cultivation of cash crops.

The last important development in this period that must be discussed is the effect on the area of the new distribution of groups and resources. With the down-movement of the Nuba as well as the settlement of Arabs, a new situation arose in which land rights had to be defined. The result of the British policies in this field was that the pastoral Hawazma who migrated through the area received no land rights, but had to negotiate agreements with the local inhabitants to be allowed to use pasture and water. For the sedentary Arabs, the British solved their problem partly by opening up new areas for cultivation, partly by drilling wells and building *hafirs* (dams), and partly by giving the new settlers ownership rights in these areas, to avoid mixing Arabs and Nubas in Nuba-dominated areas.

This system, designed to avoid conflict between groups, was further strengthened by the introduction of Native Administration. As we have seen, it ensured the various tribes the right to administer themselves through their own tribal leadership. The same structure of leadership was also effective in working out agreements between tribes about the use of resources, of pasture and water rights. Through their leaders, the Hawazma pastoralists negotiated acceptance by the Nuba and other Arab groups of their use of pasture and water. They did the same with the tribes of the Upper Nile in the Southern Sudan. For the settled populations, the tribal leadership became an important mechanism for solving land disputes between groups and for negotiating acceptance of territorial borders.

The period of independent Sudan, starting in 1956, represents a continuation of earlier developments towards greater commercialization of the economy, but with new factors appearing that provided new opportunities for people in the Liri region. In the field of wage labour, the development of an industrial sector in Khartoum in the early independence period provided people with new opportunities for seasonal migration (El-Hassan, 1976).

The civil war between the north and the south created a great demand for soldiers in the northern army, and many Hawazma boys enlisted during this period (Osman, 1986). Duty in the southern war zone brought good incomes, and the money was invested mostly in animals. At home, the prices of cotton were good, and finally, the demand for meat in the Arab world raised the price of animals. The first decade of independence was thus economically a fairly good period for the people. The number of animals grew. Some Nuba groups acquired so many animals that they took up a pastoral way of life.

But there were also new developments related to the state's involvement in farming. In 1967 cotton growing was organized in a new way. The cotton company stopped being only a distributor of seeds and a market organization, and was given development tasks (Kerzani, 1983). The Nuba Mountains Agricultural Production Corporation was formed to

1. Increase productivity, reduce cost of production and provide crop protection through research and extension services.
2. Improve economic, social and cultural standards of farmers through the provision of drinking water, social services, rural development and the encouragement of cooperative movements.
3. Encourage group farming, mechanized farming and the organization of rotational rules for the cultivation of cotton and sorghum.

These ambitious aims were not followed up with an adequate administrative structure. Rather, the result was a drastic drop in cotton production.

This led the Nimeiri regime to go even further in 1970 by introducing the concept of "modernization schemes". But they were also a failure. During the first years the results were a reduction of cultivated areas within the schemes by 55 per cent, whereas administrative costs increased by 81 per cent (ibid.). Thus a crisis in this sector started that was to last into the 1980s. People were reluctant to grow cotton because of bad prices. They were constrained in their sorghum cultivation because of the rules of rotation within the schemes. Productivity was also low on the schemes due to late planting of the crops, which in turn was related to mechanical problems with the fleet of tractors. Studies of these schemes in the late 1970s and early 1980s showed that the traditional sector was at least as productive as the cotton schemes and that the reluctance on the part of the farmers to participate was indeed a rational choice (Manger, 1979).

A second direct state intervention in the agricultural sector was the introduction into the southern Nuba Mountains of large-scale mechanized schemes, comprising farms of 1,000 acres each. These were administered by the Mechanized Farming Corporation (MFC) established in the 1960s. The first scheme of this type in the Nuba Mountains was Habila, in the late 1960s, and in our region further south, the Beida scheme was established in 1976. Unlike the modernization schemes, these types of schemes were not aimed at small-holder farmers, but rather at people with capital who could afford the investments. There is an initial fee to the MFC in order to get a scheme, and then a yearly rent. But the real cost lies in clearing land of trees and buying mechanical equipment (tractors and discers). Furthermore, the management of such schemes, with all the capital involved, the organization of hundreds of wage labourers and the marketing, is way beyond the competence of the local farmers, be they

Nuba or Arab. It was the *jellaba* who most effectively exploited this opportunity. In 1979, only seven of thirty-seven farms in the Beida scheme, were owned by non-*jellaba*, and none of them was operating (Manger, 1984).

The impact of the schemes can be seen on several levels. Economically they have been a success for their owners. The profits reaped by the traders are considerable, and this success has created increasing income differences in the region. In 1979 I did a calculation of the distribution of incomes on the schemes among the owners and the workers, i.e. between capital and labour, and found that 53 per cent went to the owner and 47 per cent to the workers (Manger, 1979). Since the owner was one or two persons and the workers several hundred, there was a dramatic difference in the distribution of incomes from the schemes. The traders' position as the dominant economic group in the area has been further strengthened and the workers, i.e. the local farmers and poor migrants from the south, remain poor, with the schemes providing a vital additional income for these groups.

Ecologically these vast schemes also have an impact. First, due to the lack of rotational practices, the farmers let the land deteriorate; when this happens, they get a new scheme. This is contrary to the rules of the MFC, but experience shows that the rules are not applied. The schemes thus appear to be places of agricultural mining rather than agricultural farming (Shazeli, 1980). The schemes also take up large areas that were previously part of pastoral migration routes. To remedy this, the MFC has made special corridors for the nomads to pass through the scheme areas, but it becomes a problem towards the end of the dry season, when some nomads start their movement northwards. This is the time of localized early showers of rain. For people and animals moving along the corridors it is very difficult to resist the temptation to move their herds across the farms in search of pasture and water at a time when the strain on the animals is great. At this time there may still be some grain left that awaits threshing on the farms, and this the animals then eat. This has led to fighting and court cases.

Escalating conflict

The situation for the traders, farmers and pastoralists has thus changed through the period of independence. The scheme sector and the general expansion of the commercial sector during the Nimeiri regime has helped the *jellaba* to dramatically improve their position.

For the majority of cultivators the development schemes have been places of low paid wage work (i.e. the MFC schemes) and places of decreasing interest (i.e. the NMPAC schemes). The main bulk of small-holder cultivation has thus remained within the traditional sector, using

Figure 3. *Local administrative system, 1972–86*

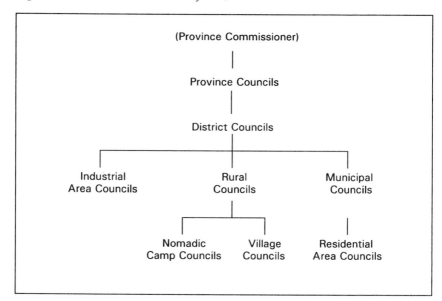

traditional hoe-technology and traditional crops. The income from these local activities has been supplemented by labour migration outside the area; but, on the whole, people remain in the low income categories and have to pursue a number of economic activities to survive.

Most pastoralists have also made losses during this period. They have lost grazing land, and the environmental problem affects the productivity of the herds. A few rich herd-owners have been able to go into the scheme sector, investing surplus herds in tractors; but they remain a small minority.

Ethnic contacts have increased. The Nuba and Arab groups and the *jellaba* are now all operating in the plains areas and are in direct contact with each other as neighbours, employers and employees. In addition, new groups have entered the regional scene. The West African pastoralists have come during the last decades, and so have an increasing number of Southern Sudanese who have either sought wage employment on the schemes or have been brought to the schemes by the traders going to the south seeking workers. In the contemporary situation the ethnic picture is thus more complex than before, which is a situation one might expect would generate conflict.

The situation is further complicated through the demographic developments in the region. Over the last decade the area has experienced a high population increase. While the population in Rashad District grew

3.7 per cent in the period from the 1955-56 National Census to the 1973 census, the growth rate between the censuses of 1973 and 1983 was 6.8 per cent. The growth of towns was also significant, with the total urban population increasing five-fold between 1955 and 1983. This dramatic change cannot be related to demographic processes within the region alone, but is concerned with people migrating into the district. The immigrants are partly coming from drought-stricken North Kordofan where the ecological crisis is more severe, partly from the Southern Sudan, where poverty and, more recently, civil war is pushing people out. Another development is related to the nomadic groups. Their migration routes have traditionally gone through the mountains, but due to the difficulties at both ends of the routes, the pastoralists spend longer periods in the Nuba Mountains, thus adding to the problem.

All these developments are putting the southern Nuba Mountains under severe strain. The causes are complex, involving several ethnic groups engaged in a number of economic activities, and are related to developments in other regions, away from the focus of this study. Although the problems have been building up for several decades, they have become particularly acute since the 1970s. This is partly because the environmental problems have been paralleled by significant political difficulties. This is related to the breakdown of an administrative system that facilitated contact between groups and also facilitated the distribution of resources between them.

In fact, the number of conflicts has increased, as the possibilities for solving them have decreased. This is related to the abolition in 1971 of the Native Administration system. People's Councils were introduced to which people were elected according to democratic procedures. This change has placed groups other than the old Native Administration (essentially rural) leaders in central political positions. The new system is biased in favour of the settled populations, as their opportunities to elect their representatives are better than those of the nomads.

For the nomads the new system of the 1970s has resulted in a loss of influence in regional politics and, therefore, also in fewer opportunities to secure their interests in the region's resources. They lose court cases about trespassing; they have to accept the encroachment of West African pastoralists on their traditional pasture areas. The increasing number of conflicts arising from this situation take dramatic turns, with villagers covering water points that the nomads use (as happened in el-Gardud), burning pasture areas, and expelling nomads from the areas of the modernization schemes (as happened in Um Dual).

Among the settled population, the elite groups of *jellaba* and some Arab elites have benefited from the system through their participation in its most profitable activities, notably the scheme sector and trade. Their economic position has given them political influence, through which they

can protect their interests vis-à-vis other groups. But the majority of settled people also experience an increasing marginality and have problems
with securing their livelihood. They end up in debt-relations with the rich
groups and through such relationships become supporters for these
groups in the political field.

When the political crisis culminated in the civil war in the early 1980s,
the Nuba Mountains also became involved as an area bordering on the
conflict areas of the Upper Nile Province. One significant aspect of this
political crisis is the ethnic, or cultural one. The major north–south crisis
is expressed in the Nuba Mountains through a conflict between groups of
Arabic origin and the indigenous Nuba groups. Such problems are escalating due to the environmental problems and famine.

Effects on the Liri scene

One expression of the increasing rate of commercialization and the shift
between groups can be seen in the developments within the trade sector
in Liri. The investments in mechanized farming schemes have made the
Liri *jellaba* leave their involvement in consumer trade. This has opened a
new field of investment for those people who have success in their own
traditional adaptation. A good cash crop, wages etc. help people to create
small surpluses. The most common way to invest small surpluses is in
petty trading, and many people are doing that. Further success can now
be converted into a larger trade in consumer goods, operating from a
permanent shop. The general picture, then, is no longer a simple
dichotomy between subsistence oriented farmers and pastoralists versus
the *jellaba* commercial groups. It is rather a complex setting in which most
groups have become deeply involved in the commercial process and are
looking for investment possibilities to further improve their positions.

Thus a major development in the Tunguru market from 1980 to 1984,
when I paid my last visit, was the growing number of small shops (*koshuq*)
being erected outside the market place. The sites have been planned and
are distributed by the Rural Council and any person with capital can get
a license and a site and build his own shop. In 1984 there were 17 such
shops made of zinc in the market. Another interesting fact is the ethnic
heterogeneity the list of traders shows. There were 7 *fellata*, 2 Lafofa, 5
jellaba (sons of traders who are learning to become traders, or the shop is
rented out), and 3 local Arabs. Trade in consumer goods is thus no longer
an exclusive *jellaba* activity, but has become an open field for anybody
with some capital. This development is politically sanctioned from the
highest level, as the granting of trade licenses is no longer tied to requirements about how much capital a trader should have, or owning a house,
etc. Today it suffices to pay the fee (£S17) to become a trader and to get
a site for the shop.

Apart from the petty traders, there are women tea- and coffee-sellers in the market place. They all belong to the local population, most of them coming from the Arab population. In 1984 there were nine such tea-sellers and their work is also a reflection of the increasing number of people who frequent the market and the more intense activity there. The activities of these women are, therefore, an important part of, and a result of the process of commercialization.

The developments outlined above have resulted in an increasing economic differentiation between people. There are winners and losers, some become rich, others remain poor. But at the same time there are important socio-cultural changes following in the wake of commercialization. There are tendencies towards profound changes in the internal structure of households and in the organization of social and economic life in the villages. New relationships between people emerge. The husband—wife relationship is changing. The people who are successful in their economic adaptation become agents of change, not only by offering new economic activities but also by becoming representatives of new lifestyles.

The interplay between such processes of commercialization, which open new economic possibilities for people, and the requirements these possibilities set for specific identity management strategies, serve as important contexts for our further discussion.

2. The Hill people

We have now come to a more detailed discussion of how the Lafofa have adapted to and been affected by the general developments outlined in Chapter 1.

LAFOFA AS A CULTURAL TRADITION

We know that the Lafofa migrated to Liri towards the end of the nineteenth century, and settled in the mountain village that is called Lafofa. Today there are some 400 inhabitants in that village, living on a small plain some 200 m. above the plain proper. Most of the Lafofa have, however, moved down from the mountain and are today found in villages along the foot of the mountain and in some regional town centers. But several decades ago the situation was different. Many more people lived in the mountain village, depended on a system of intensive cultivation and had only limited contact with the plains population. It is to this mountain village we shall now turn and try to reconstruct a picture of Lafofa life as it went on in the early parts of this century.

To get a first impression of Lafofa society, we shall start by looking at some early ethnographic accounts of the Lafofa and the picture they present of Lafofa cultural traditions. What we want to do then is to sketch some of those basic elements that defined unity and solidarity among the Lafofa. Such internal solidarity depends on "those shared cultural characteristics which serve to bind together society", particularly "those shared symbols and symbolic acts which represent and give recognition to existing social units" and "the shared understandings" and "the countless similar behaviour patterns and similar material manifestations of behaviour which characterize a people" (Orans, 1965:4–5). I do not believe, however, that this is the totality of Lafofa culture or that such an entity exists at all. My purpose is to combine different types of data to establish *some* interconnections that may lead to an understanding of *some* basic premises for Lafofa life, thus indicating ways through which Lafofa culture was practiced and transmitted. This is important for my later discussion, in which I shall try to show how the dynamics of change must be sought in the changing connotations of the various elements contained in the "traditional" culture, not as symbols only, but rather as containing bodies of knowledge about the world.

BASIC ELEMENTS OF SOCIAL ORGANIZATION

The Lafofa belong to the matrilineal belt in the Nuba Mountains (Nadel, 1947) and Seligman, who visited the area in 1910, had the following to say about the Lafofa system of kinship

> This system is so directly in harmony with what we know of the social organization that it is tempting to look at it as a type system, associated with matrilineal descent sociologically but with bilateral descent for the purpose of blood relationship as far as incest is concerned, and to suppose that the other Nuba systems have deviated from it owing to foreign influences. (Seligman visited Kurundi, Amira, Eliri, Talodi and Tumtum of the southern Nuba and it is compared to these systems that the Lafofa systems seems like a type system. Author's comment). The chief characteristics of the Lafofa system are: all cousins are siblings, and no cousins may marry, all the ascending generations are either "fathers" or "mothers" except the mother's brother, and there is a close social bond between mother's brother and sister's son. (Seligman, 1932:382–3)

Descent and kinship

Matrilineality was expressed in an ideology descent of placing the descendants in the mother's line as a unilineal group. The unity of such a group was expressed at several levels. A basic notion of unity for people within the same matrilineage was that they came from "the same womb" (*botton wahid*). This expression could be used for people being born of the same mother, and of sisters; but it was also an expression that could unify the whole lineage. This wider usage should be understood on the basis of the Lafofa kin-term system.

It should be noted in particular that the same term is used for brother and sister (*imbie*) and Seligman gives the following example of how this was used: A man will often say "This is my *imbie* (brother)," and when asked whether he and his "brother" were born of one mother or begotten of one father he may answer "Neither" but that his mother and his "brother's" father were *imbie*. On being asked whether the parents were true sister and brother he may again reply, "No, but their respective parents were *imbie*." Very often the genealogy cannot be traced, although the relationship is remembered ... (Seligman, ibid.:381). Through such a classificatory kinship system, relations over generations are grouped together as being of the same kind, i.e. are treated as if they were sibling relations and thereby from the same womb.

To a significant extent the matrilineal kinship system also organized important relationships and directed behaviour among the Lafofa. The relationship between a mother's brother and a sister's son was particularly important. It is underlined in the kin terminology in which one

Figure 4. *Lafofa kin-terms*

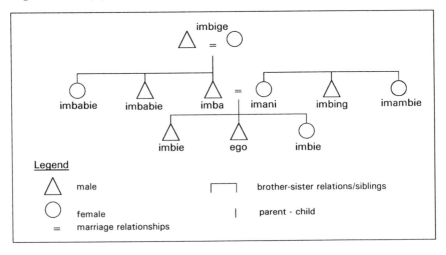

single term is used for the two (*imbing*). In everyday life this relationship was expressed by the young boys spending a lot of time with their mothers' brothers and staying in their houses from the age of about seven or eight. Similarly, after a young man's successful hunt the mother's brother should get a quarter of the meat, which was a lot more than what should be given to the boy's father. If one of them became sick, the other would bring the sick person to a healer and would pay for the treatment. At the death of a mother's brother his weapons would be divided among his sister's sons. They, on their side, should provide animals to be slaughtered at the funeral. Both men and women were buried with their maternal relatives, in "lineage graves". It is important to note here that we are not talking about specific persons, as mothers' brothers. The classificatory system grouped together many people as being of the mother's brother-type. To understand the actual relation between a specific mother's brother and his sister's son other circumstances must also be considered, as we shall do later.

Marriage

Marriage among the Lafofa was regulated by exogamy rules. Seligman's rather cryptic remark that the Lafofa have "bilateral descent for the purpose of blood relationship as far as incest is concerned" implies the existence of incest rules that prevented marriage between cousins. This also relates to the classificatory Lafofa kinship system. All cousins are termed siblings (*imbing*); and since father's siblings and mother's sisters are classified as mothers and fathers, their children cannot be married. Marriage was thus not possible as long as there was an *imbing* relationship between people. This of course depends on people's memory, and it leaves room for manipulations over time. According to Seligman, the Lafofa lineages were shallow ones, and relations were not remembered for more than three generations, thus making this system workable. But as long as the Lafofa were living on their mountain plain and did not leave the mountain to make new villages, all marriages were from within the mountain community, the in-laws thereby also being nearby.

Selection of ritual experts

The matrilineal principle was also one important basis for the selection of ritual experts among the Lafofa. The most important and powerful of these was the *rain-maker*. He was a man of great dignity possessing powers deriving from his maternal ancestors to bring rain.

From Seligman's presentation we understand that it is *Geberatu* who is the strong power from whom contemporary rain-makers draw their power. Geberatu was a real person, living around 1850, and in the Lafofa tradition he was the man who led the Lafofa from Tikeim to Liri. With time he also took on importance as a "spirit" from whom the powers of later rain-makers came. The spirits of the predecessor became immanent in the new expert while he was quite young. At that time the possessed person would stay away from the house during the night, returning in the morning. A mother would find her son gone during the night, and this was interpreted as if the spirits took him away to teach him the secrets of his position. He would then be brought up with the present rain-maker and be taught the secrets of rain-making.

Apart from the rain-maker there were also other departmental experts who operated according to the same basic principles. Power was transferred in the same hereditary way, but through different lineages. There were experts for each of the important crops. They would keep some sacred seeds in their houses, which they would share with the people at the time of planting. They were to be mixed with ordinary crops to secure a good harvest. Traditional healers were also important, as they cured different types of sicknesses, some of which were caused by witchcraft. Finally, there was an iron expert who made iron bracelets that were used by the sickness experts (Seligman, 1914:120).

Although spirits relating to ancestors were the active forces in Lafofa daily life, working through the chosen experts, the Lafofa also held a belief about a deity. The focal point of the universe was "Kalo", a high God who created all things but who was relatively passive in terms of affecting daily life. Such impacts were believed to belong to the lesser spirits, with whom the rain-maker and other experts communicated.

Figure 5.   *Genealogy for Lafofa rain-makers*

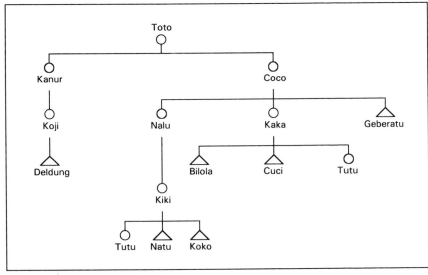

Source: Seligman, 1932:377

Becoming social persons

The most important institution regulating any male person's life, and providing him with people to cooperate with, was the *age-grade system.*

The Lafofa had two age-grades, *kamenai* and *tembing.* The first denotes a man who can marry and thus one who has become a man, the second an old man. The Lafofa age-grade system is thus a simple system, not like the complex systems we see elsewhere in the Nuba Mountains (e.g. Nadel, 1952; Rottenburg, 1988). Still it functioned as an important marker of change in status for the people involved

The transition from boyhood to *kamenai* was surrounded by elaborate ceremonies. At that age young boys would spend the rainy season taking care of cattle and would live in cattle kraals (*kwere*). At the end of such a period of seclusion a dance would be performed by those involved. To take part in this dance a boy had to have undergone three periods of seclusion, i.e. three rainy seasons. This dance was called *kamelai* which comes from the word *kame*, the Lafofa term for a boy who has had his first child, denoting that he is then a man. After the dancing that ends the seclusion, the boys decorated themselves and returned to the village, where each of their mother's brothers would beat them with switches. The following day they also whip each other, later to be treated by their future wives.

The young men who went through this ceremony together stood in a special relationship to each other and made up an important solidarity group. They would hunt together, help each other in daily work, and, if no incest rules prevented it, would marry each other's sisters. These young men would also dominate the ceremonial wrestling matches that were held after harvest time.

For the girls there were also such markers, signalling the change from childhood to womanhood. Unlike many other Nuba societies (Nadel, op.cit.) there does not seem to have existed any seclusion ceremonies for Lafofa girls after their first menstruation. But Seligman indicates that ceremonial wrestling matches for girls may correspond to the ceremonial beating of the boys. At that particular time the girls also had their bodies scarred. After a girl had her first child, she would not wrestle again, but in connection with that first pregnancy more of the face and body would be covered with scars.

In contrast to the transition from childhood to adult manhood and womanhood, marriage among the Lafofa was not a major ceremonial occasion. Young people arranged their own love affairs; and if two people decided to marry they would tell their parents who would normally accept this. The girls would go on living with their mothers until after the first child was born. In this period the husband would work for the wife's people. Such *bride-service* is common in matrilineal societies. After the first child was born, a house would be built for the couple on the land of the boy's people. The beer for this work was provided by the wife's side, although many others would take part in the actual building. In case of divorce, which was frequent, the man would keep the house; while the wife would move to the house of a new husband, taking the children with her.

Birth was not extensively celebrated. When a first child was born, a sheep or goat was slaughtered, but not for any ceremonial reason; instead to supply food for a feast. More important was the act of taking a copper ring to the sickness expert. He would put it in the ashes of his "sacred fire". The ring was then put on the foot of the child to protect it against dangers in life.

Lafofa children, like many other Nuba children, are given names according to their birth order, i.e. whether they are the first child, second and so on. A first-born boy is invariably called Koko, the second Kafi, the third Tia, the fourth son (if no girl is born) is given the female name Tutu, and the fifth Nalu. For girls the same sequence is Kaka, Toto, Koshe, Kiki and the fifth Nalu. Such series of names start with each marriage, i.e. they apply to children born by the same woman. Any person may thus have several sons and daughters who have the same name. Apart from these names, children are also given nick-names that are used to distinguish them.

Death dramatizes the matrilineal relationships as we discussed above and brings specific relatives into action. The body is put in a lineage grave together with the deceased maternal relatives. The living maternal relatives provide an animal to be slaughtered and supply beer to be drunk during the period of mourning that follows the death.

The above description highlights some aspects of culture and social organization among the Lafofa as it was observed in the first half of this century. The features described underlined the system of descent and kinship, and the performance of central rituals. In this, which for the time being I shall call "traditional Lafofa culture", we see the close relationship between mother's brothers and sister's sons, and how lineage membership affected marriage and death. Similarly, there are religious leaders who perform important tasks in relation to economic life and also sickness and general daily life. All this took place within a religious and ideological context which formulated important beliefs about how the universe was organized. In the following we shall pursue some contexts in which we can see how the principles outlined above function within a context of other Lafofa activities, particularly focusing on the economic level.

SOCIAL ORGANIZATION AND THE AGRICULTURAL SYSTEM

The organizational principles within the Lafofa social organization also provided important contexts for local economic life. While all Lafofa stayed on the mountain, they practiced a quite intensive system of cultivation with multiple linkages between agriculture and livestock and labour-intensive dry terracing. This intensive cultivation evolved in the context of population pressure on the confined mountain plateau.

In spite of the fact that the Lafofa kept animals such as cattle and pigs, they were predominantly agriculturalists; and crop production was the mainstay of their economy. During the rainy season the Lafofa were occupied with the cultivation on two different fields. These were the *house fields* and the *near fields*. Both types were found on the mountain itself, or along the very foot of the mountain. This was because the Lafofa always had to be ready to defend themselves against attacks, the best defence being to return to their own mountains. On these fields men and women cultivated sorghum of different varieties, planting it in May and harvesting it in October–November. The harvested grain was tied in bundles and put on the roof of a *rakuba*, which is a roof supported by poles, used to provide shade. This public display of the harvest was talked about and was the basis for the classification of people as good or bad farmers. Grain was threshed in small quantities for consumption, but the main part of the threshing normally started in January. Apart from using grain for their own consumption it was used to make beer to mobilize labour and on other occasions.

We have seen that the Lafofa matrilineages are significant units through which important aspects of Lafofa social organization can be understood. In this section, we shall look at how such lineages provided contexts for the Lafofa to operate in agriculture. The discussion thus relates to the corporateness of Lafofa matrilineages.

The corporateness of the matrilineage was expressed through common residence, access to land, common mobilization of labour and common defence (which, as we shall see, is closely related to the way labour is organized). Clan matters were handled by clan elders who enjoyed considerable influence and made up a "court" to which disputes were referred.

In the following we shall concentrate on how this regulated access to the basic production factors, land and labour.

Access to land

For the Lafofa the transfer of both house fields and near fields was defined by their matrilineal descent system. Members of the same matrilineage would live near each other up on the mountain, within an area defined by a water course, a hill or some stones. Within such an area, the owner of a homestead would also cultivate around his house; and when he died, the person taking over the house would also take over this house field. Access to and ownership of house fields was thus obtained through the processes deciding residence. The ideal was to be brought up with a mother's brother, and to take over his house. But with the classificatory kinship system this meant that this relation could be used for many different people. Although matrilineal relationships defined access to fields, they did not determine which people actually would be involved, and, therefore, what the actual relationships were.

This pattern of residence would also be influenced by marriage and divorce. As we saw earlier, the wife's family built a house for the new couple, but did so on the man's land. The ideal situation would then be for some sister's son to move into the house to be brought up there, the children of the couple moving elsewhere to their matrikin. In case of divorce this pattern could be broken; and children would stay on with their fathers, the land of the matrilineage thereby also being used by the sons of men, who belonged to different matrilineages.

This flexibility was also the case for the transfer of near fields. Such fields could be obtained from the side of the mother as well as that of the father, and fields could be obtained at different times during a person's life. The transfer of land was thus determined by the opportunities available to several people. The flexible system permitted pragmatic solutions to the land problem by allowing people in need to get the plots they re-

quired. Nadel (1947) describes similar systems among the Masakin and
the Korongo, who are also matrilineal tribes in the southern Nuba Mountains

> Now it is clear that this fluid rule of paternity precludes a strict or perma-
> nent distribution of kinship groups and (matrilineal) clans. When young
> men marry, they build themselves new houses close to the home in which
> they were brought up. If they had lived with a mother's brother, this would
> foster the spreading of the clan in the same locality; if they lived with their
> father, houses representing different clans would spring up side by side.
> Successive generations may do different things: the relationship of man
> and place admits of no continuity. This irregular design must deeply affect
> the life of the family and individuals. Brothers may grow up together, or
> may live in different localities. Indeed, to the individual the place and com-
> munity in which he finds himself in adulthood is little more than an acci-
> dent, the outcome of a fifty-fifty chance. We must add that in this system
> of adoption the mother's brother is sometimes replaced by the maternal
> grandfather or the mother's mother's brother. A third and fourth chance
> of adoption and domicile thus enter in the calculation. The haphazardness
> which we discovered in the composition of the tribe and its communities is
> typical already of the nucleus of the social system. (Nadel, 1947:274)

Among the Lafofa the place of residence is not "the outcome of a fifty-
fifty chance" as Nadel asserts it is for the Korongo and the Masakin. The
factors influencing residence patterns, and access to house fields, did not
operate at random. Rules of descent as well as the various opportunities
available to the people involved influenced the choices that were made.
Taking over the site and the house fields that go with it depended on the
situational context at the time the transfers took place. The spatial consequence of this would be different from that of the Korongo and the
Masakin. They are tribes living in their home territory, with many villages spread out there. For the Lafofa, these processes would take place
within the mountain plain on which they were living, i.e. within one village. It would thus be possible to maintain day-to-day relationships, also
in cases of differences in choices of fields.

Labour power

A prominent feature among the Lafofa is the extensive use of communal
labour. During the cultivation season, work parties were seen every day.
In the dry season communal labour was used for threshing, for collecting
grass and branches for house-building and for the house-building itself.
The ordinary type of work party among the Lafofa was the *nafir*, which
is the same as we know from elsewhere in the Sudan and in Africa (Netting, 1964, 1965; Barth, 1967a,b; Gulliver, 1971; Nypan, 1971; Storås,
1976; Shazeli, 1980). A man will invite his neighbours and relatives to

help with a certain piece of work. The organizer will provide beer, or food for those who do not drink. The amount of food and drink may vary according to the amount of work and, consequently, on how many people will have to be invited. It is, therefore, not possible to generalize about the size of a work party.

This ordinary work party is not the only form of group labour found among the Lafofa. Two other types, which are much more elaborate in their organization, were also found. The more important one is an institution called "*hakuma*" which literally means "government". The second one is called "*maliki*" which comes from the Arabic word "*maliki*" meaning civilized. The two are somewhat similar in organizational structure.

A *hakuma* will be a group of around 30 people, who hold different grades in an organization. These grades are organized in relation to each other, forming groups of equals who will sit together when there is a gathering. It is thus a highly formalized type of work organization. With a *maliki* the elaborate grade system is absent, and the ritualized occasions are not there, but basically it works like a *hakuma*.

An important point about these labour institutions is that they are not indigeneous Lafofa institutions but seem to have been adopted as a result of the Lafofas' contacts with other groups. The background of the *hakuma* is not clear. It might be related to the *baramka*-institution which is found among the Baggara Arabs (Arber, 1940; Cunnison, 1966). These groups of men form a club for the ceremonial drinking of tea, and usually sing songs in praise of sugar. From the Baggara groups it may have spread to the other groups of the area, also to the Nuba, where it was transformed to an institution for agricultural cooperation

> ... the Awlad Himeid who came north to Habbania country in the rains picked it up and took it south where it caught on among the serf-like communities of the southern Kawahla at Errio, at Werne and at El Liri. (Arber, op.cit.:142)

When the British Administration heard about the tea drinking, they forbade the gatherings because they might have some potential for mobilizing resistance against the British. This could be related to the fact that apart from being labour institutions, these groups probably also served as defensive units of the Nuba. People always took their weapons with them to the fields, and they worked in lines which, if attacked, could quickly become lines of defence (Vicars-Miles, 1934). And indeed, among the Nuba there was a tendency to militarize the institution. Arber mentions that in El Liri the titles were those of Turkish military grades, like *Bey* or *Mufattish*; and the *baramka* itself was called *turak*, later to be changed to *hakuma*.

It is also possible that the *hakuma* might be related to the *ghazwa* organizations. These were raiding parties organized by rulers in the early Sultanates in order to collect slaves. Once outside the sultanate these *ghazwas* were organized as strict hierarchies, using titles from the royal house. Later this organization developed into the *kubbaniya*, the major difference being that firearms were used in the latter (O'Fahey, 1977, 1980). This likelihood of connection is further substantiated by the fact that the word *turak* denotes a unit within the Turkish army.

The *maliki* is known from the Tegale Kingdom. Arber says that it evolved among Arabized Nuba from the simple work party (*nafir*) of the pure Nuba and its rules strikingly resemble those of the *baramka*. Among the Lafofa the difference between the two is in the number of participants, the use of grades and the use of sanctions.

Without reducing all the complex labour organizations found among the Lafofa to a mere functional unit within the intensive agricultural system, one implication was surely that the making and repairing of terraces, weeding and harvesting as well as house-building and other tasks were made easier through the mobilization of such groups. The reciprocal nature of the mobilization of such groups also secured a distribution of labour within the society. This did not mean that there were not economic differences. There were individual differences, and they were shown in the bundles of grain seen on the *rakuba* roofs. A surplus of grain could be used to make more beer, and would thus enhance the status and prestige of an individual who could treat the workers lavishly. The work-parties also operated on the borders of Lafofa territory, where people were susceptible to attacks from enemies and thus also served in a defence function. Because such labour organizations were recruited from within the matrilineal lineages and from people living on lineage land, the work groups were very much part of the basic system of social organization among the Lafofa, as sketched out above.

THE RITUAL CYCLE AND AGRICULTURE

Apart from providing access to production factors, the system of social organization and culture described above was also closely tied in with the agricultural system through the ritual cycle. We saw that cattle and cattle-kraals played a role in the age-grade ceremonies, but the major parts of indigeneous ritual practices and religious life were largely bound up with the agricultural year. As we shall see, there are differences in how people participate in various phases of the ritual and agricultural cycle, a fact that can lead us to some important basic concepts in the Lafofa cultural tradition.

The importance of rain

Rain-making and the activities of the rain-maker were an important pre-requisite for starting cultivation among the Lafofa. Seligman describes how the rain-making ceremony of the Lafofa of *jebel* Eliri was preceeded by elaborate secret preliminaries. The site of the rain-making was at the foot of *jebel* Eliri, where there are ruins of a sizable settlement

> Here are certain features traditionally associated with Geberatu: the foundations of his house, showing remains of large pots and his granaries; his grave, indicated by a depression in the ground with pieces of wood at the sides of a narrow hole, and at the side of this a slab of rock bearing the foundations of a hut in which Geberatu performed the rain ritual. These remains were excessively holy, and it was only after prolonged negotiations that we were allowed to visit the spot. (ibid.: 399)

Based on descriptions by MacDiarmid, a missionary working in the area in the early century, Seligman was able to give the following description of the ritual itself

> When rain is due people come from their villages to the rain-maker's hut, carrying branches of trees. They dance and call on the rain to fall. The rain-maker then goes into his hut, where three fairly large white stones (mone'e), brought many years ago from the old home in the Tikeim hills, lie in a row. The rain maker spits on his finger and places it on the ground near the central white stone, next touching his eyes, the front of his neck, his navel and his big toe. The assistant kills a large pig provided by the rain-maker and brings the blood in a gourd inside the hut, placing it on the ground near the central stone. The rain-maker touches the blood with his finger, which he carries to his eyes, neck, navel and big toe. Then he takes the gourd of blood, comes out of the hut backwards, and turning around throws the blood into the air. (ibid.:401–2)

This ceremony is also the sign for people that cultivation may start, and they proceed to sow their seeds. But the participation of the grain-expert is also important. He will mix grain of his own with that from people before they take it to their fields to plant. This is, however, done individually, not in elaborate ceremonies as was the case with rain-making.

Links between the harvest and concepts of fertility

The harvesting of grain was also very important for the Lafofa, but not as an expression of the role of rain-making but rather as a metaphor expressing basic relations between people. This can be seen by the ways the harvest period is also the period for the important transition ceremonies and ceremonial acts that celebrate life.

First of all, harvest time was also the time for *wrestling*. For boys the wrestling matches seem to be only a sporting event celebrating their strength and manhood, but for girls this was also related to ritually signalling the transition from being a girl to becoming a woman. There was no seclusion of girls in the granary as is the case among the Masakin (Nadel, 1947), but wrestling and the scarring of the body were symbolic expressions of the same transition. The link between fertility, women and grain also came out later, when the grain was to be threshed. Only women would carry threshed grain from the threshing ground to the granary. The harvest, wrestling and scarring went together for girls to signal a transition from girlhood to womanhood. It was tied to basic notions of *fertility*, which can be linked to the harvesting of the life-giving sorghum.

The same period, i.e. after the rainy season, was also the period for the important transition ceremonies among boys. For boys the *age-grade* system was the basic integrative element. Through the ceremonies, basic elements of the matrilineal system were dramatized, as well as fertility, through the act of the boys being cared for by their future wives.

Ritual and meaning

The two examples of how the agricultural system was tied to the ritual cycle differ significantly. The rain rituals were basically secret and depended on the expertise of the rain-maker. We have seen earlier that this expertise is transferred through a matrilineage but that its transfer is closely related to spirits arriving in a person's dreams and taking him away to teach him, thus further underlining secrecy and the process of special selection. The knowledge on which a rain-maker acts is thus partly part of a relationship between this individual and the holy spirits, partly a socialization process in which an older rain-maker trains the new one. The details of the ritual are thus sure to change and vary over time, although the basic outlines of the acts may have stayed the same. But the relationship between the rain-maker and the people is one in which the rain-maker mediates between them and the spirit world to bring the rain on which life depends. Rain-making thus underlines and is dependent upon a certain cosmological order.

Rituals relating to harvest time are quite different. The elements of secrecy are not there, only public rituals in which people themselves are the actors and in which they celebrate relationships that tie people to each other, not to the spirit world. The links to reproduction and fertility are there, the transition ceremonies that mark important changes in social status are there, and the realities contained in the matrilineal system and matrilineages are also present. I am not saying that this bears no relationship to the spirit-world or that notions of fertility may not be related to cosmological notions, but that by the very way these rituals are socially organized, they imply very important differences in the messages they contain. They thereby also underline different existential aspects of Lafofa life.

The role of grain

Sorghum was the basic subsistence crop among the Lafofa, and its availability would determine the future of the Lafofa. Grain also served as an idiom for various other important values among the Lafofa. We have said that the display of grain on the roof of the *rakuba* indicated the presence of a good farmer and thus had to do with notions of rank. Apart from being cooked as porridge for subsistence, grain was also made into beer to be used on different occasions. As in other African communities, beer among the Lafofa was important in mobilizing labour for cultivation, house building and other activities that require communal efforts (see e.g. Manger ed., 1987). Beer is also important to those who make it, i.e. the women. It is important for a woman and wife to be a good beermaker, thus acquiring rank in the female sphere. But beer was not only significant in such economic contexts. Beer was an integral part of all the ritual occasions that we have described. I do not have details on the use of beer during the period we are discussing, but we may safely state that beer serves as an important idiom on several levels of Lafofa society.

The agricultural process thus provided not only subsistence products but also basic idioms for the expression of Lafofa unity and solidarity, thus further underlining the close interconnection between the economic and socio-cultural levels of society.

CONCLUSION

Throughout this chapter we have tried to build a baseline picture of important elements of Lafofa social organization, ritual organization and economic life. We have seen that in a traditional Lafofa context these levels were closely linked together. Following our basic assumptions, this should mean that such patterns of integration also contain messages for the Lafofa about themselves, their role and place in the world. These messages are transmitted through rituals, but also through everyday activities. The form of these messages depends on the participants, the ways messages are transmitted, i.e. the modes of communication, and the tasks involved. We do not have specific information on how this earlier way of life was conducted among the Lafofa; it is a reconstruction of earlier ethnographic accounts and interviews with people. Our next step is to provide a picture of the contemporary Lafofa society as I observed it during my fieldwork in the late 1970s and early 1980s.

3. Contemporary Lafofa society

The "traditional" pattern outlined in Chapter 2 has undergone many changes since Seligman described it, after his visit in 1910. On my arrival at the Lafofa village in 1979 it was not difficult to elicit information about traditional culture that shows that people still entertain parts of its ideology, although the changes were also very clear. The following is a summary account of some persisting and other changing features.

SOME MAJOR SOCIO-CULTURAL CHANGES

The matrilineal ideology still exists among the Lafofa, although the organizational implications of this ideology has changed. Cousins are still termed siblings in the Lafofa kin term system, but today they may marry. One important exception to this is that it is impossible for a man to marry his mother's sister's daughter. Children of sisters are still considered to be from the same womb (*botton wahid*) and marriage therefore, would be incestuous.

The introduction of a bride price instead of bride service, and the elaborate ceremonial occasions around marriage are new developments. Marriage customs common in Central Sudan have been introduced since the 1940's, giving marriage an economic dimension it did not have before, forcing young men to earn money to pay for it. Building the couple's first house has become the responsibility of the young man, not of the bride's family as before. Divorce has also become more problematic, since a man will not get back his money if he himself initiates a divorce. A woman who wants to get a divorce has to pay back twice the sum of the brideprice which, with the sums involved today, is virtually impossible unless she is helped by relatives.

The position of the rain-maker and other departmental experts has declined in importance, although they are still significant. Rain is no longer believed to come as a result of the rites performed by the rain-maker, and he does not perform them in public any more. Rather, rain comes at the will and mercy of *Allah*, and it is the *faqi* who mediates between *Allah* and the people. Similarly, today the traditional healers have "competition" from those *fuqara* (pl.) who can cure through reciting the Koran, or offer protection by making amulets. Although there are illnesses that are still treated by *kojors* (those related to witchcraft), these experts no longer possess as central a position among the Lafofa as in the past. The age-grade system has also declined and is no longer a living in-

stitution. The seclusion periods no longer exist, and the transition ceremonies are the Islamic ones of namegiving, circumcision and marriage.
The *faqi* provides the spiritual leadership on such occasions, not the *kojor*.
The decreased importance of the *kojor* also means that the harvest rituals
which he initiated and which were a celebration of fertility have disappeared. So have the initiation ceremonies which were held at the same
time.

The changes outlined above give an impression of the direction of
change. However, we also see a complexity of changes that are not clear-
cut at all. The organizational consequences of certain elements have
changed, but the notions of the traditional elements are still there, influencing the "new" features. Important positions have changed content,
but there are still actors holding the position. We are thus not confronted
with a clear-cut process of change, with a uniform momentum. Rather, it
seems that change is differential and that old and new patterns coexist.
We shall continue, therefore, with a more detailed description of some
important cultural markers in order to better view the complexities of the
changes.

THE NEW IMPORTANCE OF MARRIAGE

For any Lafofa boy who wants to be married, it has become a major economic investment, because the various items required for a marriage
amount to sums that are well above what can be earned locally. The following case shows this.

Increasing costs of marriage

The introduction of bride-price instead of bride-service and the ceremonial occasion itself are new elements that give marriage an economic aspect that it did not have previously. The bride-price and, especially, the
things that are required from the groom for the bride's family (*schela*)
have increased significantly in recent years; and the total costs of a marriage are now above £S300, for a first marriage. This expense makes it
necessary for young boys to engage in labour migration for several years
in order to save enough for this occasion. Marriage is therefore influenced by Arab and Islamic customs, as well as by economics, in the sense
that the development of prices for the goods involved directly influences
the cost of marriage. For the Lafofa, this development is strongly dominated by the inflationary process in the Sudanese economy.

The case of Mosa Keki

Mosa wanted to marry a girl in the village, and the first approach was made
by his representatives to the relatives of the girl in January 1980. At that
time Mosa was in Khartoum on wage labour. In order to start the talks at
all the bridegroom's side has to present some gifts. In this case it consisted
of one goat, a bottle of oil, two *rotl* (1 l. = 2,25 *rotl*) sugar, one *rotl* coffee, two
rotl onions, one *rotl* dates, one bag of candy and 1/2 a *rotl* of tea. When this
was paid the bridegroom's representatives were allowed to come back for
more serious discussions about a wedding. In this discussion the bride is
represented by four females, and they get £S10 each for being there. This
is paid by the suitor. In addition there is need for an offering (*karama*),
which in effect is another round of gift-giving. When the representatives of
the bridegroom went to negotiate, they brought with them one goat, a bottle of perfume, rice, candy, onions, salt, soaps, squash, dates, gas, sugar,
flour and tea. The women were not satisfied with the amount; and more
coffee, sugar, flour, soaps, onions and rice had to be brought. The total expenditure amounted to about £S20 (including the goat).

When this gift was accepted, the goat was slaughtered and the meat eaten;
and the real negotiations could start. These negotiations last for hours and
there is a very hot bargaining around each item. The Lafofa themselves
talk about the bargaining as "wrestling", referring to the real matches that
they have towards the end of the rainy season.

The result of these particular negotiations was as follows

haq al talaga	for the divorce	£S25
fatah al khasm	to open the mouth	£S25
haq al niswan	for the women	£S90
haq al mosba	for the finger	£S10
haq al adan	for the ear	£S10
haq al agrab	for the scorpion	£S10

Of the £S170, £S70 could not be paid at once and was to be paid after
another year in Khartoum. This money is used to give the bride necessary
things like a bed. In addition to the cash the following items were demanded: 20 *rotl* of sugar, 4 *rotl* of coffee, 8 kg flour, rice, macaroni, 3 kg
adis, 2 *midd* dates, 3 *midd* onions, 12 bottles of oil, 4 bottles of gasoline, 3
lamps, 4 stoves, 4 bags of candy, 3 boxes of cigarettes, matches, 9 pieces of
soap, one sack of charcoal, 3 *rotl* of salt, 4 bottles of perfume, dried tomatoes, 3 bottles of squash. On top of everything comes the goat that will
be slaughtered on the wedding day, which it was decided would be two
weeks later. This is the length of time the bride's representatives give those
of the bridegroom to get the items agreed upon.

On the wedding day the things were carried by a group of people through
the village; and after the items have been checked and accepted, the wedding ceremony itself can start. In addition to the expenditure on the
negotiations with the bride's family, comes about £S5 for the holy man

(*faqi*) who says the Islamic blessing. Furthermore, one has to be prepared to entertain guests in one's house during the three days that the wedding lasts. These guests do, however, give a gift of money on the first day of the wedding. In Mosa's case this amounted to about £S25. On the fourth day, in the evening, the bridegroom returns to his own home; and this also calls for food and drinks. The groom will bring a goat, while the people of the bride will give grain and beans. Altogether, then, the wedding we have described cost more than £S300. Most of the money Mosa had earned as a labour migrant in Khartoum. But, as we saw, some money had to be paid the following year. Apart from the money from Khartoum, Mosa also sold a gun belonging to a MoBr, which fetched £S75. He also wanted an ox from another MoBr to cover all the expenses before he returned to Khartoum, but this MoBr refused to give him the animal he asked for.

What this case shows us is that the direct costs involved in the marriage of a first wife makes it into a major "investment" for a young Lafofa man. He has to combine money earned from wage labour with incomes from things that he can sell locally. Loans from other people are also common. The increasing costs of marriage have made it necessary for young boys to engage in labour migration for several years before they can afford to marry. Boys are, therefore, in their twenties when they get married, whereas the girls are ready for marriage after their first menstruation.

Marrying a second wife, who has been married before, is much less costly. Such a marriage can be arranged for about £S20–30 and can be managed through locally earned incomes. There were several second marriages during my field periods. Only one second marriage, that of Mohamed, the largest of the three shopkeepers in the village, was with a girl who had not been married before and he paid the price of a "first" wife. Normally the costs are relatively low, so it is not necessary for men to go to Khartoum on wage labour to get money for a second marriage. The procedure for the marriage negotiations is similar for both types of marriages, but women who have been married before cannot expect to raise the same amount as in a first marriage.

The establishment of a domestic unit is thus a matter of increasing cost and a first marriage forces young men to engage in labour migration for several years before they can marry. The cost aspect of marriage entails that men make similar adaptive choices. As migrants they are subject to similar influences, as well as making friendships that are significant when they are in the village, especially as they sanction each others behaviour. A second marriage does not have such implications.

Effects on divorce

To get a divorce has also become increasingly difficult as the cost of the marriage has increased. A man who initiates a divorce will not get back anything of what he paid. A woman who insists on divorce will have to pay back twice the sum her husband paid. Such a divorce has to be made effective by the local court (*mahkama*) or the Islamic judge (*qadi*) who comes to the area once or twice a year from his headquarters in Kalogi. With the sums involved such a divorce becomes virtually impossible without the help of several relatives. This point is underlined by the observed divorces of Kaka and Koshe.

> Kaka is an old woman who was the third wife of her husband. She complained that her husband never brought her clothes or any food, e.g. grain from his harvest. She refused to stay in his house and moved to the house of her MoBr. The husband did nothing to make her return; he only wanted his money. He was paid £S8 by Kaka, and the divorce became effective. Kaka later remarried and moved to another village to live with her new husband.

This short case may be compared to one which involved the village trader. The problems arose after he married a second wife.

> After the second marriage, his first wife, Koshe, who was without children, was unwilling to stay in the house, and spent more time in the house of one of her brothers. After some time Mohamed brought her to the local court. His argument before the court was that Koshe did not come to his house to make food, instead she went out alone in the evenings and did not return to the house. He accused her of having another man, but said that if she would return to the house and do her duties, he would make no further trouble. Koshe answered that the reason for the trouble was that she was ill. She wanted to go to the doctor, but Mohamed had not been willing to go with her. She wanted to go with one of her brothers, but Mohamed had also been unwilling to pay the bill.
>
> The court ruled that if this was the case Mohamed should go with her to the doctor. If he did not, she should notify the court. If he did go with her, Koshe should move back to the house. Koshe refused to accept this solution, as she claimed Mohamed would never accept it. Mohamed said he would, as he was sure his wife was not ill. Ahmed, Koshe's brother, also spoke at this point, and tried to minimize the problem, and said that as "brothers" there should be an acceptable solution to all parties. He brought Koshe with him to talk to her. His intervention and that of four other brothers did not, however, change her mind, and Ahmed had to report to the court that she refused any solution but divorce.
>
> The court again appealed to Koshe, saying she had nothing to complain about. She was not beaten, she got nice clothes (she was nicely dressed in a dress and *taube*), and Mohamed was a respectable man. But to no avail. So the next step was to decide on what should be paid back. Mohamed had paid £S20 as the brideprice, and £S120 to the women. A total of £S145. Mohamed argued that he wanted £S290 as was the custom, but the court stopped him and said that in this case his wife would pay £S145 first, and later they would decide on the rest. Koshe was given seven days to pay the

money. She said she had £S9.50 with Mohamed and she wanted this money back. He answered that he had given her brother £S1,50 so he would give her £S8.00 only. Ahmed confirmed this. She had a bed that was hers in the house. It had been bought for the £S120 and belonged to the bride. Apart from this she claimed nothing.

On the following court day she had paid £S100. She and her brothers had not been able to collect more. The court decided to wait until more money came in before they continued with the case. On the mountain Mohamed later told me that Koshe could do as she pleased. Without paying the £S290 she would not be legally divorced, and could not get another man. He would just wait to get his money back.

Growing local concern about costs

The increasing costs of marriage were not only a problem for the Lafofa but were of general concern for people in the area. The Islamic judge was working to reduce the costs and had succeeded in parts of the area. The Lafofa in the mountains was the last group of people who had not yet adopted a standardized cost. However, in June 1981 there were meetings where people came together to discuss the problem and agreed on a fixed sum of £S203 for all weddings. The argument was that the girls had to wait too long before they could marry, and this increased the risk for pre-marital contact and illegitimate children. Another argument, among the men, was that the negotiations that took place before the marriage gave women too powerful a position. The men had to obey the will of women. The fixed sum would mean an end to the negotiations altogether and would, therefore, solve this problem. The final argument was that the young men had to stay too many years in Khartoum. Some did not return. However, the sum of £S203 is still a lot of money, and the agreement will not radically influence the migration patterns of the young boys. It does, however, confirm our statement above, that the establishment of a domestic unit is now basic for the Lafofa and that its economics strongly influence the development of marriage and divorce. An agreement that would remove the negotiations before marriage would also affect the Lafofa in another way. This is related to how marriage negotiations have been regarded as wrestling matches, thus indicating something about how the Lafofa bring notions about group relationships into new situations.

MARRIAGE CUSTOMS AND RELATIONS BETWEEN GROUPS

The new marriage patterns among the Lafofa also have implications for the relationships between the marrying groups. As we saw in Chapter 2, the in-laws never came from one's own family. The fact that people from the same social group may now marry means that the status of kinsman (e.g. mother's brother) and the status of in-law (e.g. father-in-law) may coalesce in the same person. This is a qualitatively different situation from the one where kinsmen and in-laws came from different groups because of the incest rule. The traditional Lafofa notion of incest, however, still prevents the marriage of a boy to his mother's sister's daughter, the reason being that such people come from the same womb.

But even if people who earlier belonged to the same clan may now marry, the concept of the spouses belonging to two different groups is still important, and important elements of Lafofa culture are intertwined in this fact.

For instance, in the marriage negotiations, the two sides are represented by people who decide on the actual amounts of cash and goods that are involved in the marriage. Men represent the groom, women the bride. Such negotiations are occasions for displaying great rhetorical skills, and people openly evaluate the performance of the participants. People call these negotiations *wrestling matches* and when discussions about certain items go high, they talk about them as "good wrestling matches".

Such negotiations may also continue on the wedding day itself, when the things are presented to the bride's family. On several occasions I witnessed how earlier agreements were not accepted and new "wrestling matches" took place. The importance of this to people was dramatized once when some migrants brought a piece of paper on which the amounts were written down. These migrants were attending evening schools in Khartoum and were proud of their ability to read and write. When the disagreement started on the wedding day, they brought out their paper and claimed that this was the end of the matter. They were strongly critizised, and people said they were spoiling the fun.

My interpretation of this type of incident is that although marriage has changed and now involves rituals it did not have before, the content of these rituals reflect notions of traditional Lafofa culture. Wrestling was a thing related to transition ceremonies; it took place at harvest time and was related to the clan system. It is thus a suitable idiom for the Lafofa to use to interpret what is going on between the two intermarrying groups.

But wrestling is not only an idiom that functions for the Lafofa as a group. It is also an activity that signifies part of the Lafofa identity and must be related to the processes of integration that the Lafofa have been going through. In the following section we shall discuss some of the changes relating to wrestling.

WRESTLING IN A CONTEMPORARY CONTEXT

Ceremonial wrestling was related to the harvesting season and for girls it also represented a transition ceremony. Today wrestling exists in Liri, but for boys only. No girl ever wrestles. But the wrestling for boys has also changed. Traditionally it was organized according to membership in the matrilineal descent groups. People from the same descent group should not wrestle with each other. Wrestling today is organized regionally, with a number of villages making up one team. A Lafofa living in a plains village will, therefore, wrestle with someone from the mountain because they belong to different teams.

Wrestling has also become a sport for the Arabs in Liri and is, therefore, an event with many new elements. Old men watching these modern matches sometimes interfere in the fights to point out that two wrestlers should not fight since they are related. They are always turned down by the cheering audience and come away shaking their heads over the modern decay of the sport. Wrestling is an example of an old sport still practiced, but with a new cultural content and new participants. It continues, however, because it still celebrates important values of strength and manhood that are shared among the Lafofa and the Arabs.

If we compare this to the development of female wrestling, we see that it has disappeared altogether. Again I want to relate this development to the opening up of Lafofa society towards the surrounding world and the need to express basic human qualities as they are expressed in that world. Although Arab women certainly differ in the way they live, depending on the ethnic group to which they belong, a basic notion is, however, that they are not like men and that the celebration of the male ideals about bravery and strength does not apply to themselves. Rather, men are considered to be superior and should protect women. Female wrestling thus is in much stronger opposition to such notions of womanhood than male wrestling is to the Arabic notions of manhood.

NEW RITUAL LEADERS

New ritual leaders have also entered the scene among the Lafofa. In the past the most important and powerful of such *kujors* was the rain-maker. He was a man of great dignity possessing powers deriving from his maternal ancestors to bring rain. The rain-making ceremony was partly secret and partly public. For his service to his community the rain-maker had his plot cultivated for him. Apart from the rain-maker there were also departmental experts who operated on the same basic principles. There were experts for each of the important crops. They would keep some sacred seeds in their houses, which they would share with the people at the time of planting, so they could mix them with ordinary seeds to secure a good harvest. Sickness experts were also important, curing different types of illness, some of which were caused by witchcraft.

In the General Introduction I described how the position of such ritual experts has been challenged in this century by the activities of Muslim missionaries from Islamic brotherhoods, *tariqas*. In Liri the *Qadiriyya* is the dominant sect, and within it is the *Makashfiyya* branch with its center at Gezira. The history of this *tariqa* in the southern Nuba Mountains in general and in Liri in particular goes back to the beginning of the present century, and is related to the coming in 1906 of *Sheikh* Bernawi who had been initiated by the *Makashif*. He travelled around for many years, teaching the locals, as well as intermarrying with them. Eventually he settled down in Liri and built his *mesid* (local center) there. After his death his son, *Sheikh* Abdel Bagi took over as religious leader and has continued up to the present.

Around these leaders a group of followers developed, some of them being Lafofa. These local converts became propagators of the new religion among their own people. The most important one for the Lafofa was *Sheikh* Hassan, who died one year before I first came to the mountain. During my fieldwork a new local *sheikh* took over.

The *faqi* performs the Islamic rituals at important events like namegiving, circumcision, marriage and death. They also operate as healers to the extent they have been given power (*baraka*) to do so. Apart from operating in these capacities the Lafofa *faqi* keeps the drum called *noba*, which is at the center of the ritual dancing (*dhikr*) on Thursday and Sunday evenings. The dancing itself takes place outside the house of the *faqi* and attending the dance is an expression of belonging to the group of believers. The place where the *noba* dance was held was moved to the house of the new *faqi* during my stay, an occasion marked by an offering (*karama*). However, this novice *faqi* was not yet performing the above mentioned rituals. They were conducted by an established Lafofa *faqi* from a village near the eastern market place, al Khor.

The position of the rain-maker and other departmental experts is thus of reduced importance, although they are still there. Rain is no longer believed to come as a result of the rites performed by the rain-maker and he does not perform them any more. Rather, rain comes at the will and mercy of *Allah*, and the *faqi* is the person who mediates between *Allah* and the people.

Similarly, today traditional healers also experience "competition" from these *fuqara* who can cure through reciting the Koran, or can offer protection by making amulets, and so on. Although there are illnesses related to witchcraft that are still treated by *kujors*, these experts no longer possess as central a position among the Lafofa as they used to. We have also seen that the transition ceremonies are new. The *faqi* provides the spiritual leadership on such occasions, not the *kujor*. The decreased importance of the *kujor* also means that the harvest rituals, which he initiated and which were a celebration of fertility, have disappeared. So have the initiation ceremonies which were held at the same time.

The center for the Liri *Qadiriyya* is the *mesid* where *Sheikh* Abdel Bagi

Figure 6. *Relationships between present Lafofa leaders*

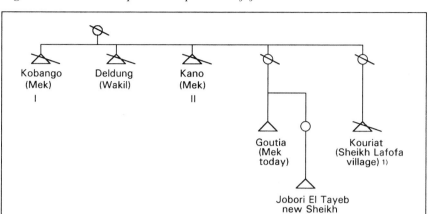

1) Sheikh Kouriat died during my field period and was replaced by Jobori.
People referred to Jobori as Kouriat's sister's son (*wad ukhtuh*).

lives. All the *faqis* in the region come to him regularly to pray and to pay
their respect and listen to his teachings. At the important Islamic festivals
(*Id al Dahia, Id al Fitr*) there are big ceremonies with a parade and dancing. The dervishes, in their patched clothes dominate this dancing, but
other people also join in and become part of the trance-like activities.

The *Qadiriyya* in Liri thus appears as a ritual and organizational unit
with the head *sheikh* at the pivotal point, and smaller *sheikhs* as his representatives. This network of dervishes is very important for teaching illiterate people about Islam. The teaching of Muhamed and the content of
the Koran are transferred through direct contact between a *sheikh* and his
followers. Thus, to a Lafofa, being a Muslim means going to the places
where the teaching goes on, be it at a *noba* dance, a *karama*, a wedding in
the village or the *mesid*.

SUCCESSION TO OFFICE

The succession of political and ritual leaders among the Lafofa was also
framed within the matrilineal system of descent. We saw in Chapter 2
how the ritual experts were related through the matriline (Figure 5). Figure 6 shows the same for the political *mek* and *sheikh* leaders.

Here we see that such leaders are also recruited from the same descent
line as the traditional ones. We saw in Chapter 1 that the *mek* is a tribal
leader parallel to the *omda* among the Arabs and that he is responsible for
the collection of the animal tax. Before 1969 he also had judiciary powers
within a tribal system with a *nazir* on top and *mek* and *omda* below. The

sheikh has a village based position, with powers to judge in minor disputes and to assist in the collection of taxes. Both positions are related to the old Lafofa system.

There has been a change in the authority of leaders as well as in the qualities relevant to their recruitment. Before, a good leader needed spiritual gifts to make him a rain-maker; he was a good leader in tribal wars. To-day knowledge of Arabic and an understanding of the ways of the government are more important assets. In the political life of the Lafofa today, the rural council system is also a factor and recruitment to that system is totally different. In the Lafofa village council the migrants are dominant, in particular the largest trader in the village is most active. This council is responsible for organizing the distribution of government quotas of sugar and flour. The council also forms "problem solving committees" that may challenge the authority of the village *sheikh*.

CHANGES IN ECONOMIC LIFE

The agricultural system described in Chapter 2 was an adaptation to specific socio-political and economic developments in the southern Nuba Mountains during certain historical periods. In a contemporary context they change and deteriorate as distinct systems of agricultural intensification. Today the Lafofa have to a large extent left these activitities. They have adopted the more extensive cultivation practices found among their neighbours. One major factor contributing to this is the general pacification of the areas. Governments in this century have been able to guarantee the safety of the inhabitants in a different way from earlier ones. Groups like the Nuba have been able to move into areas in which they can start more expansive cultivation again (see Roden, 1972, for details about the Nuba Mountains, McCown et.al., 1979, for similar trends within the broader Sudan savanna belt). In this changing context the factors making up the Lafofa agricultural system also appear in new forms.

Today, with less pressure on land in the mountain, the rules for land transfers are less critical, and people have a wider variety of choices of fields. The most important alternative now is, however, the opening up of *far fields* down on the clay plain.

Land is not scarce on the clay plains in Liri. Inheritance is, therefore, not of crucial importance in obtaining land there. A son may clear his own fields independently of the ones of his father. Since the area is declared and understood by all to be Government land, one does not ask anybody's permission to clear it. This situation obtains of course, because land is plentiful. Further north, in the Central Nuba Mountains where population densities are higher, all land has been used and there the transfer of plots and also of far fields, is important (Roden, 1972; Salih, 1983).

Most often people from the same village cultivate fields close to each other. They feel more secure if they can go together with neighbours. Another advantage of being together is that people can arrange small work parties in the fields. Since clearing land is hard work, a person may prefer to cultivate a field which is already cleared. He may ask someone he knows who is not working his field whether he could borrow the field, or he may contact a relative. In the first case a cultivator is always in danger of being told to leave, but in the case of a relative one is more confident of being left in peace. No compensation is paid for borrowing fields.

The far fields are planted and harvested later than the mountain fields. Various types of sorghum are planted together with sesame and beans. Some years ago cotton was an attractive cash crop, but today this production is approaching zero. The people who cultivate far fields stay there for several days at work time. They build shelters to stay in and try to get relatives and others to come and help them during peak periods. After the grain is harvested it is brought back to Liri in lorries.

With the far fields we also find that land use differs from what is common in the mountain. A plot is cleared, all the trees are cut, and the grass is removed by fire (*hariq*-cultivation). Fire breaks are made round an area to prevent the fire spreading. When the new grass is coming up, with the first rains, a fire is made to remove both the old and the new grass. After this, the land is ready for planting. There is a general rule in this system that the fallow period should last as many years as the land was cultivated. The normal cycle is four years cultivation, four years fallow. But people usually clear a field, rectangular in shape. After a number of years the user leaves one part of it fallow and expands at the other end. The far fields receive a certain amount of manuring since the cattle nomads come to the area towards the end of the cultivation season. The cattle can, therefore, feed on the stalks that are left on the fields and simultaneously leave their waste.

Um Gudja, east of the mountain, was the first place where the Lafofa cultivated far fields after it was safe for them to do so. Some Lafofa also settled down there, forming the Um Gudja village together with some Kenana Arabs in 1971. Due to declining soil quality, the mountain Lafofa have now shifted to other places. One is Abu Feda, on the western side of the mountain, along the Talodi road, where five Lafofa men have their fields. The other is Al Baida where another five Lafofa were cultivating within the scheme area of a *jellaba* who did not do much cultivation. During my field period this scheme was sold and the Lafofa had to stop their cultivation. They then returned to house and near field cultivation in their mountain village.

Figure 7a. *Lafofa village: Residence pattern*

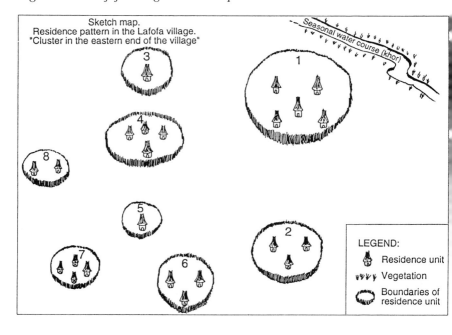

Figure 7b. *Lafofa village: Kinship relations*

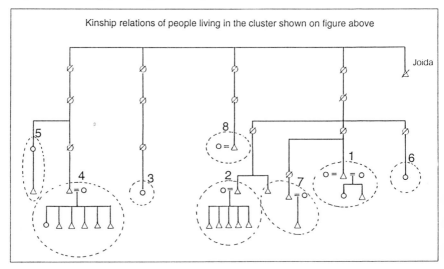

CONTINUITY AND CHANGE IN THE MATRILINEAL SYSTEM

One characteristic of the Lafofa system, when people were still living on the mountain, was that they were organized in corporate clans, the corporateness being expressed in common residence and access to house fields and to labour through communal work groups organized on the basis of clan membership. The same groups were important in joint defence.

Today members of matrilineal clans do not live in the same areas as the clans are no longer localized. This development has been caused by down-migration to various villages in Liri and elsewhere. This settlement shift as well as the commercialization of economies has brought a decline in communal labour and more emphasis on wage work. The growing importance of far fields has also brought changes. On the mountain people still acquire house fields and near fields through descent and inheritance. With far fields, which are now economically the most important types of fields, different principles operate. Until now land has been plentiful and new far fields could be opened when needed. Over time such plots will probably be transferred from father to sons. Communal work groups could not be mobilized to work on these types of fields.

This process of change has been most profound for those of the Lafofa who have moved down from the mountain village. On the mountain we still see elements of the old system, and through a discussion of these elements we may be able, not only to see a disappearing system, but also to see how the system is changing.

Residence

In the Lafofa mountain village, the matrilineal principle is still important for understanding residence patterns as the following survey of one locality in the village shows.

Figures 7a and 7b show the matrilineal principle and how rights passed between men, but through women, within this system. The important link was that between mother's brother and sister's son. The people in my case all refer to *Joida* as the one who provides them with a legal right to their area.

Compound 1. Idris took over his house from an elder brother who died (Enkato). Before this he had been living down on the plain. At the time of the English attack he moved down with his father, only to move up again at the time of his marriage, when he found a girl from the Lafofa village. Since his brother died, Idris moved into his place.

Compound 2. Umbelle was living with his mother where Kiki (No. 6) now has her house. He got a place next to this house and built his own there.

Compound 3. Kaka is a leper. She lives together with another female leper in a house some distance away from the others.

Compound 4. Demri was brought up at the place where he is now living. He was taken from his father's house to be with his maternal relatives.

Compound 5. Koshe is an old woman who lives alone in her house, next to Demri. Her only son is in Khartoum and has not been back for many years.

Compound 6. Kiki was living with her mother until she was old enough to marry. Then she moved to her husband's village down on the plain. When her mother died, she moved back to her mother's place which at that time was available, and she has lived there ever since. At the time of my field-work her daughter's eldest son was staying in her house to learn to discontinue suckling.

Compound 7. Mohamed has married recently and has had to build a house for his new wife. He was allowed to do it on the plot of Koko, who is a leper, where he was brought up as a child. As a small boy he lived elsewhere in the village with his father. When he married, he built his house at the place of his mother's mother, who had brought him up after he returned from his father. Since Koko was alone and needed assistance because of his illness, Mohamed was allowed to build the house on his land.

Compound 8. Enkato is an old man who always has lived in his present place. Joida is his mother's mother's brother.

The above examples show that rights deriving both from the mother's and the father's side are valid. We see a clear pattern of how the matrilineal principle gives form to residential units in the mountain village. But we also see that the opportunities available affected the choices made. One can also acquire land away from one's area, which might be related to decreased pressure on land. Women get land with the same reference as men, but it was always underlined by the men "*ma fi niswan inda'hum ard*": there are no women who possess land. My general conclusion is, however, that matrilineal descent still affects residence. It is the down-movement from the mountain that leads to new residence patterns; the system as such is not changing dramatically.

Inheritance of land

In our discussion of residence rules we have also mentioned access to house fields because they are found immediately around the house. These plots are rather small, a few hundred square meters, and are not sufficient for a household. In addition, other fields are required. Such plots may be aquired from within the matriline, from a mother's brother, or from maternal relatives several generations ago. But land may also be obtained from the father. Women will either cultivate their husbands' plots, or land from their brothers. And as we pointed out above, "*ma fi niswan inda'hum ard*". Table 2 gives an impression of this.

Table 2.   *Access to agricultural land in Lafofa*

Name	Kind of plot	Kind of product	Source of right
Demri	house field	cereals	MoMoMoBr
	near field	peanuts	Fa
Idris	house field	cereals	MoMoMoBr
	near field	peanuts	MoMoMoBr
	near field (on plain)	peanuts	Father
Amna	field a	cereals	Brother
(wi. of	field b	peanuts	Brother
Idris)	field c	peanuts	MoMoSiSo
Koshe	field a	cereals	Husband
(wi.of			
Idris)			
Jojo	house field	cereals	MoBr
	near field	peanuts	MoBr
	near field	cereals	MoBr
Toto	next to house	cereals	Husband
(wi.of	near field	peanuts	Husband
Jojo)			
Tia	near field	cereals	Father
Kiki	next to house	cereals	Husband
(wi.of			
Tia)			
Kaka	near field	cereals	Husband
(wi.of			
Tia)			

Again we see that both maternal and paternal relatives are important, although it is interesting to note that many cash crop fields now seem to be obtained from the father. This might be the same tendency as noted elsewhere that, in processes of economic development, the economically important assets within a matrilineal system are transferred from fathers to sons (Goody, 1958; Gough, 1961). The same principle is also clear with reference to animals.

Inheritance of animals

Animals were probably of greater importance to the Lafofa in the past, economically as well as ritually. One notable change is the total absence of

pigs in the Lafofa village today. They have disappeared completely with
the coming of Islam. Cattle, however, still play an important role. Apart
from the milk they produce, they are also slaughtered for food at times
of weddings, deaths or public ceremonies. Cattle are also sold to get
money to buy subsistence products.

Cattle were part of the flow between mother's brothers and sister's
sons, thus being an asset within the matrilineal groups. Today there are
still people who receive animals from their mother's brothers, but I also
witnessed conflicts in which sons took away animals from such people.
When I asked about this, the standard answer was that "they took their
right" (*shaloo haqq'um*). To questions about whether sisters' sons could get
any animals from their mothers' brothers, even if that relationship was
strong, the answer was that in such cases a mother's brother would *give*
animals in his lifetime as a sort of "anticipated inheritance". In "normal"
cases of inheritance the father's right would now prevail in court.

With animals, then, we see a clearer development away from matrilineal inheritance towards a father–son link. This was also discussed on
several occasions in the mountain when people would recall the days
when they got their *haqq* from their mother's brothers and not as today
from their father. But in people's minds this process had already happened; they did not talk about the complexities we have seen, of the
coexistence of different principles.

Changes in the mobilization of labour

The settlement of the Lafofa on the plains has also led to a disintegration
of the communal work groups. Such changes can be seen both in the organization of the groups and the possibilities for their mobilization.

First, there is the question of who can be mobilized. For the ordinary
nafir, the people who are to work together are told to come to the one arranging the work. The organizer will ask neighbours, relatives and in-
laws. In the more formalized parties, it is mainly place of residence which
will determine what unit someone will join. Thus there are *hakumas* and
malikis from different parts of the village; and their names denote what
part of the village they represent, e.g. *hakuma teht* (down-under) which is
in the western part of the village that lies lower than the rest, as it slopes
down towards the western end of the mountain; or *hakuma LoTiro* which
is from LoTiro, the name of the northern part of the village. It may reflect the old organization of such work groups within lineage groups, but
today the membership pattern is different. One factor to interfere with
this is that the Lafofa are spread out and have fields in the mountain village and on the plain. The same goes for a man who has moved down to
the plain but who has fields on the mountain. He will join the *hakuma* of
the place where the field is. A second factor is that the people from the

Liri village further up the mountain can now join a Lafofa *hakuma*. This village is small, and the two largest cultivators in Liri are both members of one of the Lafofa *hakumas*. Thirdly, the Islamized non-beer drinkers have a *hakuma* of their own. This is a new principle for recruitment, for it is religious identity and attitudes towards beer which determine which *hakuma* one joins. Such people are often members of other work groups as well, because of the greater working capacity of those groups where the experienced elders are members.

A second important aspect is a change in the type of work the groups can be mobilized to do. Communal labour is used to collect grass and branches for houses and for the actual building work. It is used in cultivation, for planting, weeding, harvesting and the clearing of peanuts. An interesting development in the mountains is that people refuse to be mobilized for far field cultivation. People cultivating far fields can, therefore, not expect to have their *hakumas* work for them there.

Through involvement in a regional labour market, hired labour is now more common on the far fields than are communal work groups, even among the Lafofa, who still remain in the mountains and cultivate far fields, since the work group in which they belong, are of no use.

However, for those still living in the mountain village, the best way to mobilize people is still through the traditional labour parties. Since all cultivators work on their own fields, there is a limit to how many people one can mobilize at any one time. In the institutionalized *hakuma* and *maliki* organizations, between twenty and thirty persons are likely to turn up.

Those organizations are still found, but with the developments in this century they have also taken on new functions. In addition to the work they do for each other, the *hakuma* members may give each other money instead of labour. The one whose turn it is to have a party may decide that he needs money instead of labour. All the arrangements are made, the food is prepared etc., the only difference being that every member gives 20 Pt., which is the rate of one day's work, to the person involved. With 30 members this makes a total of £S6.

A *hakuma* can also serve as a saving's club. All the fines and money paid by members on various occasions are collected in a box and taken care of by a cashier. This money may later be redistributed among the members when they need them.

Women may also have *hakumas* on their own. They can work in each others' fields or provide money for each other. They do not fetch grass and branches from the mountain, since house building is men's work. Women may also be members of the men's *hakuma*; they then get their work done and work for other men on the same basis as any other member.

THE CONTEMPORARY PATTERN

In Chapter 2 we described the matrilineal descent system among the Lafofa, and tried to show how this system was at the basis of Lafofa social organization. Membership of clans secured access to land and labour, determined the succession of important ritual experts, and provided an essential context for Lafofa notions about themselves. Clan exogamy was also important and marriage was not an elaborate thing, with easy and frequent divorce. The domestic unit was a loose one. Basic Lafofa notions about the world were related to how the principles of social organization were tied to ritual life and the agricultural cycle, the inter-connectedness being expressed through Lafofa rituals.

The discussion in this chapter has not sketched a clear picture of the direction of those changes. Rather, we have seen that many traditional matrilineal elements are still operating among the Lafofa. It is also clear that there have been changes. Major changes relate to the demise of matrilineal clans as corporate groups. Today the only field in which we can recognize such corporateness is in the field of blood-money. Residence, agriculture and so on no longer have those elements. For people still living on the mountain elements of this remain, but for the Lafofa as such, their down- migration from the mountain has brought drastic changes.

With the fading corporate status of the Lafofa matriline, the hold those matrilines have on their members has also weakened. Replacing the strength of the matriline is the emerging strength of the nuclear family. Referring back to Chapter 2, we said that in basic ways traditional Lafofa society was founded on matrilineal descent, and that "womb relationships" were clearly more important than affinal relationships. The husband–wife relationship was thus clearly of secondary importance to lineage relationships. Marriage was not an elaborate occasion, divorce was easy, and the offspring would relate to mothers' brothers, thus remaining within the matriline.

Our discussion in this chapter shows that this has changed dramatically. Marriage has now become a major investment and a major occasion in peoples' lives. With the rising cost of marriage and the ways divorces are obtained, it has also become increasingly difficult. The family unit thus seems to be of greater importance now than before. This is true both in production and in defining relationships between people. The role of men and women has changed, and so have the relationships between them. All in all, the domestic unit now appears as a much more significant unit within Lafofa society than before, relations around it replacing those of the matriline in importance. In the following chapter we shall deal in greater detail with such domestic units among the Lafofa.

4. Variations in adaptive strategies

I argued in the General Introduction that one important requirement for understanding the observed changes among the Lafofa is to look at the various ways individual Lafofa participate in social and economic life and that the degree of mobility within a wider social context lends important dynamics to such processes of change. I also ended Chapter 3 by saying that the domestic unit has increased in importance. In this chapter I shall outline the empirical picture of adaptive variation between different people and different units. I am concerned with the contemporary economic integration of the Lafofa into wider socio-economic structures through cash crop cultivation, labour migration and an increasing dependence on the market. On a general level such an integration leads to processes of commercialization of the local economy and to new patterns of economic differentiation. I shall demonstrate the major effects of this process on the Lafofa who participate in the different income generating activities mentioned in the preceding chapters. Local cultivation, animals, trade and various types of schemes all represent opportunities for people to make a living. Yet we shall see that the extent of involvement in the various activities is not identical for all economic units. Some units concentrate on local cultivation, others combine this with labour migration or involve themselves in trade. We shall start with an overview of the general economic changes that have affected the adaptations of the units.

GROWING COMMERCIALIZATION OF THE ECONOMY

The cultivation of house, near and far fields has brought the Lafofa into the market sector through the marketing of their products. Cotton used to be cultivated on the clay plain and peanuts on the sandy soil on and around the mountain, and they both were important cash crops introduced by the British. People's willingness to grow the new cash crops varied. Some leaders could use hired labour and grow large amounts of cotton and peanuts and thus strengthen their position. Ordinary people cultivated limited areas, but with the increasing need for consumer goods they had to rely more and more on the money they earned from cash crops. Sugar and tea are important items in this respect. Clothes became a necessity as the Nuba changed from paganism to Islam (or Christianity). And, finally, in bad years, they also had to buy the basic food items, sorghum and beans. To get the things they needed from the market they became more and more involved in the growing of cash crops.

The implications of engaging in the cultivation of these crops varied.

Cotton was a crop totally dominated by the State and the producers had to sell their crop to Government bodies. As cotton demands a considerable input of labour, the mountain Lafofa were at a disadvantage because they lived far from the fields. They concentrated on peanuts as a cash crop. Information from NMAPC in Talodi shows that in villages where little cotton is grown, more effort is put into sesame and peanut cultivation (Manger, 1979). This crop was sold to the local *jellaba*, on the local market. Unlike the price of cotton, which was set by the authorities, the price of peanuts was related to local supply and demand and the existence or absence of credit relationships between the *jellaba* and the Lafofa. From the same traders the Lafofa bought consumer goods and the *jellaba* thus acted as agents and mediators between the traditional sector of the Lafofa and the money dominated sector of a larger economy.

Before we go on, we should mention a fairly recent phenomenon in the Lafofa mountain village, the planting of fruit and vegetable gardens. This activity has been adopted from the larger gardens on the plain, especially on the eastern side of the mountain. *Mangoes* are the most popular tree, and many people try to grow some. The importance of the garden, apart from on the economy, is for land use. They are situated in places where water is close to the surface and the whole garden is fenced in by thorn bushes. Part of the land is, therefore, cut off from the free passage that is common anywhere else in the village. Since water is close to the surface, these are places where also cattle are watered. The gardens affect the movement of cattle, and conflicts may arise when cattle tear down thorn fences. Laying down gardens seems to be on the increase among the Lafofa, and people with access to suitable land with water invest their time on this activity.

WAGE LABOUR

The opportunities for wage labour in the village are limited. The Lafofa are farmers who are willing to work for wages only in times of specific need. Then the wage is negotiated on the spot between the parties involved.

A few people have found work in the Liri market, with the police, in bakeries and as watch-men. As such jobs are limited, people are more likely to find work that is paid on a daily basis, rather than a permanent job.

Finding wage labour on the cash-crop farms of the *jellaba* has also been a possibility. In the 1970s, with the expansion of schemes in al Baida, the wage labour opportunities for the Lafofa have increased significantly. The operations on the large farms that are mechanized are preparations of the land, i.e. ploughing and sowing. Manual work is used for clearing new land, to weed and to harvest. The labourers come mainly from the

Talodi and Liri areas; but large groups of Southerners also come to get work, especially during the harvest. Among the Lafofa some men may decide to seek work together. They contact a merchant who owns a scheme and are allocated an area to work at an agreed price. They fit this work into their own timetable and give priority to their own cultivation. I once saw a group of men from Lafofa who were working in al Baida in May, but returned home to the village before they had finished in order to do their own planting. They had seen the rain fall in their home area. A person usually goes to al Baida once or twice a season. The average period a worker stays in al Baida in the dry season is sixteen days, while in the rainy season he stays for only nine days.

For the Lafofa, the development in the industrial sector in Khartoum in the early period of independence (late 1950s, early 1960s) was more important because it provided people with new opportunities for seasonal migration at a time when the Lafofa were well established in the plain villages and were integrated in a commercial economy (El-Hassan, 1976). According to El Bushra (1972), as many as 185 new industrial enterprises were established in the period 1956 to 1966, with 100 more being established before 1969. This represents a radical change from the period 1945–1955, in which only *six* enterprises of this sort were established. The attempt to create an industrial sector within independent Sudan is therefore a major "pull-factor" to explain the labour migration to Greater Khartoum.

There is thus long-distance migration, in which a majority of people go to the Khartoum area. New migrants are recruited by old ones, with the result that many men from the same village work in the same place. An example of this is the soap industry in Omdurman where many Lafofa are employed. They rent rooms together and stay together as a group all the time.

The opportunities for wage labour are increasing, on a national as well as a regional level. Thus the "pull" factors are easy to trace in the general development of the Sudanese economy. However, there are also "push" factors that make it necessary for the Lafofa to become involved in it to earn more money. These factors are related to the increasing bride price and also to general changes within the Lafofa household, through which increasing consumption needs are paralleled by the withdrawal of the wife as an independent producer. Labour migration is today widespread throughout the Nuba Mountains, but there are local variations as to why people leave and where they go (see e.g. Ibrahim and Ruppert, eds. 1988).

The general need for cash to buy consumer goods is important in this respect. With the growing degree of Islamization, the cultural practices have changed as well. Of importance to us in this connection is the institution of marriage. In the past no brideprice was paid among the Lafofa,

but we saw in Chapter 3 that with the present marriage customs a sub-
stantial amount of money has to be paid to the bride's family (£S300).
Young men have, therefore, left their villages in large numbers in order
to earn the money they need.

An important point is, however, that different people participate in
different ways in these processes of change. Some concentrate on local
cultivation, others combine this with labour migration or become involved in trade. The implications of such choices will also differ, both in
their prospects for economic success and also in how they act as agents of
change, such as those we have indicated in Chapter 3.

ADAPTIVE VARIATION AMONG UNITS

Case 1. *Muhamed Koko*

Muhamed was born down on the plain, in a village there, but he was
brought up in the mountain village, with a MoBr. He has several MoBrs in
the village, and he also married the daughter of one of them. Muhamed's
father is dead, and his mother is married to another man and is living down
on the plain, in the market village on the eastern side of the mountain. He
is the oldest of her children. A brother is away on wage labour in Khartoum
(he was not back during my periods in the area), and there are some smaller children. Muhamed has been married for two years and has an infant
son. He was away in Khartoum to earn money for his wedding, which at the
time (1978) cost him £S117.

After the marriage he and his wife lived in the house of his MoBr, who
is a leper and who needed somebody to look after him. Muhamed cultivates the area around the house on land which was earlier cultivated by his
sick MoBr. Most of the work is done by Muhamed himself. He has had no
labour party since he cannot afford it. However, he is a member of two
Hakumas, one "belonging" to his part of the village, and one for non-beer
drinkers, and has to participate in these. His own explanation of why he is
a member when he cannot make use of the labour for his own cultivation
is that he has to learn how to cultivate from the older men and that there
is a lot of fun in a *Hakuma*.

In the dry season of 1979–80 he tried to start a business as a butcher in
the village. He had saved enough money to buy some goats to slaughter to
sell the meat. The business developed fairly well, according to his own standards, but then he got involved in buying a stolen goat and the authorities
discovered that he had no official licence to work as a butcher, so he ended
up in prison for some time.

Before this happened Muhamed has taken wage labour on one of the
farms in al Baida twice, earning about £S20 altogether. Muhamed's wife
also cultivates, on land belonging to her MoMo. Her mother died just before I arrived to do my fieldwork, and she spent much time in her MoMo's
house. However, she did not return to Mohamed's house when he expected and then, as well as on several other occasions, the spouses were in

conflict. Like her husband, she is unable to mobilize any work party and is therefore working alone, with occasional help from Muhamed.

During my stay in the village this woman brewed beer on her own for sale for the first time. This was the occasion for amusing remarks from the customers, the joking indicating that she was now becoming a real wife for Muhamed. On other occasions, however, the spouses had fights; and some of these conflicts ended up at the village *Sheikh* for mediation. Muhamed was furious on several occasions when he came home to find his wife was away drinking beer with other women. He contacted her father and later her MoBr. When I was around, this was even more infuriating to Muhamed, as he claimed it was shameful to him not to be able to offer anything to a guest in his house. Without a wife there could be no tea. Such conflicts arose several times during my stay, but in spite of Muhamed's threats to divorce his wife and get another one, nothing like this happened.

The wife's version of these conflicts was that Muhamed was away very often, going to the market to drink and would never tell her where he was going or when he would be back. She was not willing to sit in the house waiting, but wanted to be with her sisters. She also complained that Mohamed never brought the things she asked for and never had any money. The household did not work effectively.

The production of this household is not big. They have a deficit from their own cultivation, which they make up for when Muhamed goes to al Baida. Due to economic difficulties, Muhamed planned to go to Khartoum again in the summer of 1980, but the problem that landed him in prison prevented this. Another possibility is that Muhamed can cultivate far fields. He has access to one field from his father, so he does not have to clear a new one, but this field is in an area which has been cultivated for a long time and is not as productive as before. Moreover, Muhamed says, the fields are too far away for people from the village to be willing to help him. This, then, would entail too much labour.

Case 2. *Tia Ahmed*

Tia has been married some years and has two children. He lives not far from his father's house and that of his elder brother. The house site is on land from his MoMoBr, and the area around the house is cultivated by his wife. For several years Tia did not cultivate in the village at all. He continued going to Khartoum for wage labour after he married. He also started cultivating far fields in the 1978–79 season. His elder brother, Kafi, (case 3) had already cleared some land there, and Tia cleared his own plot next to it. There were also some other people from the village cultivating in the same area. This is an area west of the mountain on the road to Talodi. It is a "new" area for far fields for the Lafofa, after Um Gudja in the east began declining in productivity. The presence of his brother gave Tia security for his cultivation. If he was delayed in coming back from Khartoum, Kafi would help him. Tia is also the owner of some animals, three cows with calves. One of the cows Tia has bought, the other two he got from his father, Ahmed, who has divided his cattle between his two sons, Tia and Kafi.

In 1980, Tia took up cultivation in the village. He got access to a plot for peanuts from his brother Kafi. The same year he also invested in a shop in the village, bringing the number of shops in the village up to three. After he put up the shop, Tia has not been back to Khartoum. He informed me that he would now stay in the village, taking care of his shop, cultivating some peanuts and tending his far fields. These far fields were the cause for some discussions within Tia's *Hakuma*. This *Hakuma* is the one without beer drinking, and many of the members are migrants.

In 1981 the *Hakuma* split because of disagreement about what work the members were obliged to do for each other. Those who had far fields insisted that they wanted the members to work on these fields, whereas those who did not said that they would only work in the village. This would mean that those with far fields could only make use of the *Hakuma* to get grass for housebuilding, to build a house etc., while they themselves would also have to work on the fields of their fellow members. Since cultivation is the most important activity, it was argued, this was not fair. Those who had far fields left the *Hakuma* to organize an alternative one among themselves. It would be very small, and they would have to rely on ordinary *Nafir* when they wanted something done in the village.

As I have said, Tia's wife is cultivating the area around their house, but nothing more. Tia believes in Islam and does not drink beer, nor does his wife make it. When he wants beer made for a *Nafir* he will have to go to his mother. His wife spends a lot of her time in the house, especially after Tia started the shop. As a shopkeeper, Tia is emphasizing hospitality, and people sit around the shop occasionally being treated to tea. He gets his supplies from a shop on the eastern side of the mountain and the young son of that trader visits the mountain, and is treated to tea. The wife is influenced by the new activity of her husband, especially by being more tied to the house.

Comparison

Tia is about the same age as Muhamed, but his personal economic success is strikingly different. Income from continued labour migration after marriage plays a part, as do the far fields. The cultivation of far fields was made easier by the presence of his brother on the neighbouring field. Since their father is still active on his own cultivation, they could not use his land in the village, so Tia's cultivation there is small. In spite of this lack of local land, Tia managed to create a "spiral of growth" through combining activities like cultivation, keeping animals and migration. His investment in trading is a new venture and it is too early to judge its outcome for his personal economy. We have, however, indicated there are certain changes for his wife.

Muhamed's economy is a stagnant one. He also lacks land in the village, but has not gone outside the local region to make up for this. He gets some help from his MoBrs, but they are all active cultivators who would not have the time to assist Muhamed except by coming to his work parties if he could mobilize them.

On a more general level, then, the cases point to some constraints in the adaptation of newly established units. Access to land in the village is one such constraint. This could be made up for by cultivating far fields. But then the possibility of mobilizing labour from the village would be limited. Going together with relatives or friends could alleviate this problem. Yet the individual would have to do more labour and it is also physically harder to stay out on the muddy clay plains during this part of the year.

Case 3. *Kafi Ahmed*

Kafi is an elder brother of Tia in Case 2. He is married but has no children. His wife's younger sister is staying at their house, which is next to that of his father. He went to Khartoum twice in the late 1960s, but decided to stay in the village to cultivate there. In the mountain village he cultivated some peanuts on land that he shares with a MoBr. There is no land for house fields at the place where he lives because the area is too stony. It is, however, close to a spring; and there Kafi has planted an orchard. Like Tia, Kafi got some animals from his father.

In cultivation, however, Kafi is putting most of his efforts into far field cultivation. He started out in Um Gudja, east of the Liri mountain but later went to Abu Feda on the western side, where he has now cultivated for about five years. The work there is mainly done by himself, but his father stays with him during harvest, and he hires some workers to do the weeding. The grain is brought to the market on the western side of the mountain, where it is kept by a relative.

As mentioned, Tia, his brother, also cultivates in the same area, as do five other men from the village. Kafi also has a plot in a NMAPC-scheme, not far from his far fields. He is the only one in the village with such a "scheme", and there he cultivates a small plot of cotton and sorghum. Finally, let me return to Kafi's family situation. As I said, he and his wife do not have any children. Two children were born but died as infants. Kafi spends a lot of what he earns on Islamic Holy Men so they will help to cure the wife. He was not, according to himself, thinking about taking a second wife to have children.

Case 4. *Demri Gemr*

Demri is a neighbour of Muhamed (Case 1) and a relative of his. He never stopped going to Khartoum on labour migration in the dry season. His house is on a MoBr's site. His father lives at the other end of the village. He got the place when his MoBr decided to leave the mountain to settle nearer to the market. Around the house there is some land for house fields. Some years after he married he was given a big area of land by his father, who is among the oldest men in the village and is now only cultivating house fields himself. The area is good for peanut cultivation, and Demri is concentrating on this crop. He needs a lot of labour, and cultivating in the village he can make use of the institutionalized labour organizations.

He is a member of three *Hakumas* and one *Maliki*, and makes use of all of them each season. In addition he "buys" the turn of his father in another *Hakuma*. With this labour he is able to cultivate a lot of peanuts. He will leave some of the harvest with his family, giving them some sacks to sell to get money for subsistence while he is away in Khartoum. In 1980 he spent some of his savings on a second wife. The cost of this marriage amounted to about £S25–30, i.e. substantially less than a first marriage. Demri also has some cattle and goats. He has bought two cows. One from the market village on the east of the mountain, the other from the village where he lives. The last purchase is an example of "sharing" in animals that is not uncommon. The cow with a calf belonged to an old woman. She sold the right to half of it to Demri. The progeny will later be divided between the owners. Several people have such shares in animals, and this may be seen both as a strategy to reduce the need for cash as well as a risk spreading device.

Demri's first wife cultivates land around their house, i.e. on her husband's land. She does not make beer in the house, nor does Demri drink beer. He is therefore dependent on hiring women to make beer for work parties. His second wife also cultivates her own plot on land from her mother. (She is MoSi of Muhamed's wife, Case 1.) Both wives helped Demri in the final cleaning of his peanut harvest, after a work party had done the major share of the job. The wives were paid, as Demri would give them extra sacks of peanuts. (In 1981 Demri divorced his second wife on similar grounds to those of Muhamed in Case 1.)

Comparison

These two cases are two fairly well off units. One concentrated on far fields and participates in a state scheme, the other on continued wage labour through migration. Both manage to create a surplus, proving that labour migration is not the only way one can have economic success. But Kafi's adaptation requires more labour in the periods of cultivation. He was also a member of the *hakuma* that split because some members refused to work on the far fields. He could get help from his father, and he could hire people to work for him. Demri, on the other hand, could make full use of the local labour institutions. He got land for peanuts, and the money from Khartoum made it possible for him to make optional use of this land. The opportunities available to the two units is different and their adaptational strategies vary accordingly.

The cases also provide us with an example of a man taking a second wife. The cost of this marriage is very much lower than the cost of a first marriage. It is, therefore, not necessary for men to go to Khartoum to work to get money for a second marriage. Demri is a migrant, but I also witnessed a second marriage where the man remained in the village. The procedure of the marriage negotiations is similar in both cases; but since the woman has most often been married before, her people cannot expect to get the same amounts as in a first marriage. The relatively modest cost of a second marriage makes it possible for men to make such marriages if they want to.

Turning to the women in these cases, Kafi's wife does not cultivate, whereas Demri's first wife cultivates grain on house fields belonging to her husband. Neither makes beer. They are both Islamized and play the role of a decent Islamic housewife. Demri's second wife was living in her mother's house, not moving to Demri, and cultivated land there. She also went around with the other women drinking beer, made beer herself and helped her mother to make beer for work parties. This wife and her son from an earlier marriage lived with her mother, an old woman married to a man who does not stay in the same house, but who comes in the morning and evening to milk the cows. Demri's second wife is MoSi to Koshe, the wife of Muhamed (Case 1). Koshe was backed by these older women in her conflicts with Muhamed and afterwards she could take refuge in that house.

Case 5. *Idris Enkato*

Idris is a man in his fifties. He has been married five times and in 1980 lived with his fourth and fifth wives. As a child Idris moved down from the mountain when the British attacked the village. He moved with his parents to different sides of the mountain before he moved back up the mountain after marrying his first wife. His former wives all live in the Liri area and so do all his children. When he moved up the mountain, he settled at the place of his brother who had lived there until he died.

The fields that Idris cultivates are in different places. He has an area around the house where he cultivates grain and peanuts. On parts of this land his fifth wife is also cultivating some grain. Furthermore he cultivates peanuts on a plot at the foot of the mountain. This plot belonged to his father and was his near field. Some years ago Idris also started to cultivate far fields. In the beginning he was together with his brother Kafi in a place called Lobat, where they borrowed a piece of land. The owner of the land wanted it back and the two brothers moved to Demedi where they had a right to a cleared plot from a MoBr. But the place was not suited for cultivation because cattle grazed in the area and often ate the crops. They, therefore, moved to Um Gudja, where Kafi is still cultivating. Idris cultivated there for about 10 years but gave up some 5 years ago. He told me that the reason why he stopped was partly because the land was becoming less productive and he did not want to clear a new plot and partly because his donkey died and he had no means of transport. He now concentrates on cultivating plots nearer to the village.

Idris has never been to Khartoum on labour migration. When he was young, the far fields presented the only option for those who did not have enough land. He is, however, making use of the opportunities for earning cash in al Baida.

This unit also presents us with an example of the women's place in economic life. The last wife Idris married comes from al Khor, a village on the eastern side of the mountain. She cultivates part of her husband's land. His fourth wife, however, is more active in cultivation and has a central place among the women in the village. This woman, Hammad, has been married twice. Her first husband was a leper and is now dead. By this husband she had an unmarried son who lives in the village when he is not in Khartoum. In addition to doing his own cultivation, this son helps his mother in hers. With Idris she has three living children, a married daughter, an unmarried one living in the house and a young son in the Primary School.

Hammad cultivates plots on the land of her brother as well as a smaller plot from a more distant relative. She is a good beer maker and makes beer for sale about every other month during the summer. She also makes mats for the market. The daughter in the house helps her mother regularly, both in making beer and in marketing her mats. This daughter also makes her own mats from which she gets her own small income.

Hammad is thus an independent producer, not dependent on Idris for her basic necessities. During my last field period she stayed away from Idris all the time. They had had a quarrel, and Hammad left the house to live in that of her son for almost six months. Eventually she moved back after Idris had built a new house for her. Being independent economically also makes it possible for her to contribute money or products on occasions that require it, without seeking the help of her husband or a relative, which is the fate of many women in the village. Although they are independent of each other economically, what keeps Hammad and Idris together is their common responsibility for their children.

Case 6. *Jojo Omer*

Jojo Omer is also in his fifties, like Idris, and has been married five times. He has three living children with his present wife, two boys and one girl, who are all small. In his first marriage he had two daughters who are both dead. In his second marriage he got three more girls and they are all living in a house nearby in the village. Both his third and his fourth wives are today married to other men in the village.

When he was a small boy he lived in the house of his MoBr. This house was on the land where Jojo today grows peanuts. When he married for the first time, he built his house on land belonging to another MoBr; but later on he left this place and let his MoSi take over. Today she is an old woman and looks after a big mango-tree that Jojo planted at the time he lived in that house. Jojo's present residence is the former residence of his older brother and Jojo moved there when his brother died. His brother's children are today in Kalogi, a town some distance away.

Jojo has not been away from the village on labour migration, though he once cultivated far fields, but not any longer. Today he cultivates two big plots, one with peanuts, the other with sorghum. In addition he also cultivates around the house itself. Both plots come from the MoBr with whom Jojo stayed in his childhood. He has no cattle but around 20 head of goats.

Jojo's wife Kiki, has been married once before and has four children from that marriage. Three of these children are staying in Jojo's house. This presents us with an example of how a wife may bring children from previous marriages and thereby in effect increase the consumption needs of the household. She cultivates herself, both sorghum and peanuts, on land belonging to Jojo and is thus an independent producer, like Hammad.

Case 7. *Umbelle Omer*

Umbelle has one wife only, with six sons, the eldest of whom is married. The others stay in their father's house. When Umbelle was a boy he stayed in the house of his father, Omer, then moved with his mother to her house. Later on he built his own house next to it, on land from his MoMoBr. Both he and his wife cultivate on this land around the house. Umbelle also cultivates peanuts in another part of the village on land from the same source.

Apart from cultivation, Umbelle keeps animals and has nine head of cattle. He inherited cattle from his father, together with his brother; and they still share some. They thus each keep different off-springs from the same cow. Both are considered to be well-off men.

Umbelle does not belong to any labour organization. He used to be a member of a *Hakuma*, but disagreed about some payment that he was supposed to make and withdrew. He does all the cultivation himself, with some help from his sons. Only threshing is done by a work party. Umbelle has also cultivated far fields.

As Umbelle has a large family, he and his wife do not produce sufficient. To cover expenses Umbelle sold an ox. A second ox was disposed of during my fieldwork as compensation in a homicide case. A woman killed her husband in Kalogi town. The woman is Umbelle's MoSiDa and her brother came from their home village to seek help. It was decided that Umbelle should give an ox since he had more cattle than the other brothers living in Lafofa. This ox was to be slaughtered at a peace ceremony between the parties involved, in the village of the murdered husband. This was done independently of the legal proceedings of the case.

Case 8. *Koko El Emin*

Koko, who is in his sixties and the oldest of the men in our examples, has been married six times and has two married daughters from one of his wives. The other marriages have been childless. Koko and his present wife live in his house together with the wife's SiDa whose present husband is in Khartoum. Koko occupies the place of his father and cultivates his land.

He has made use of a *Hakuma* as well as ordinary *Nafir*. He also has eleven head of cattle. Two of the four cows have been purchased. He sold one ox for a *Hakuma* celebration. Koko's wife has been married three times and has no children. She cultivates around the house, on Koko's land. Koko himself cultivated far fields before, but stopped long ago.

Comparison

In our four cases (5–8) we have seen various adaptive strategies among people who have never been to Khartoum on labour migration. The men have all cultivated far fields, showing that this adaptation has been important in order to make up for land shortage in the mountain. They all manage in the village now, thus underlining our point that the economic adaptations and the combination of resources change with time. Access to land may improve, the building up of herds of cattle also provides an important economic resource. Finally, the regional labour market may be exploited to get wage work.

As for the women, we see they are all producers, and they all make beer. Their economic position is, therefore, more independent than that of their younger sisters. At this age, both men and women may have been married several times, when the brideprice was considerably lower than it is today. They are thus examples of the traditional female adaptation of independent production that is disappearing among younger women.

CHANGES IN THE PRODUCTIVE ROLE OF MEN AND WOMEN

We have seen through these cases that the way people adapt varies according to *age*. Older men and women seem to manage on their mountain cultivation only. The men have been engaged in far field cultivation before, but have terminated this and manage today on near fields and house fields. This adaptation seems to be normal for men above 50 years of age, and is related to the lack of opportunities for other than local cultivation. In the 1960s the possibility of labour migration developed and men under 50 years of age have taken part in this or have at least had the option of doing so.

For the women there is also a difference in adaptational choices that is related to age. Older women are full producers to a greater extent than their younger sisters. The old women cultivate sorghum and peanuts on house fields as well as near fields, whereas the younger ones seem to be confined to house fields only or do not cultivate at all. This difference cannot easily be correlated with changes in the economic opportunities available to women. No new option like labour migration for the men has appeared. The changing female role should, therefore, be seen in relation to men's changing activities as well as within the framework of a general household adaptation.

What emerges from such a procedure is that households differ not according to age only but also according to their basic adaptive strategies. Although the people above 50 have adapted in roughly the same way, those under 50 vary in their choices. There are young people who try to manage on mountain cultivation alone. Others combine migration with cultivation in the mountain and still others choose the "traditional" adaptation of combining far field cultivation with mountain activities. However, all the men had worked as migrant labourers, mostly in the Khartoum area. There is thus an increasing tendency towards greater incorporation in the commercial sector among younger units, a tendency manifested by more involvement in wage labour and trade, which are "modern" activities. In the following we shall look at some factors affecting this.

THE NEEDS OF THE HOUSEHOLD

The basic diet of the Lafofa consists of a porridge made of sorghum, with various kinds of sauces (meat, vegetable, milk), sorghum beer and a stew made from sesame and peanuts. Some of the products needed can be cultivated locally, the most important of which is sorghum. A grown up consumer needs about 240 kg a year. An assessment based on the information collected shows that the average size of what I have called budgeting units consist of four persons. In a year they will need 960 kg of sorghum to cover their needs. The average result of the production of sorghum is 443 kg, which is below the required minimum. If we add the income of peanut production (converted to grain equivalents), we see that the potential amount of sorghum at the farmer's disposal is 1,345 kg. Such an average unit thus produces a surplus of 385 kg. However, there is a large variation between the various units and they should be considered individually. I shall return to this later on. The important point to note is that the production of peanuts, the cash crop, seems to be very important to the subsistence of the Lafofa.

Another important item of consumption is beans. They are the basic ingredients in the sauce that goes with the porridge. The Lafofa grow beans but often have to buy more, especially towards the end of the dry season.

The remaining important items of comsumption all have to be bought from the market. Oil, onions, salt, red pepper, dried tomatoes, tea, coffee and sugar all have their place in the Lafofa diet and they have to be bought for money. People are, therefore, in need of cash. I have made an estimate of the cash needs per day for a Lafofa family (based on interviews and observations) and it varies between 50 pt. and 75 pt. (the price of grain is included in these figures). This means that the cash need for consumption in only one year will be from £S180 to £S270. If we subtract what they cultivate themselves, i.e. sorghum and beans, the need will be 15 pt. to 40 pt. a day or £S54 to £S144 a year. In addition to these expenses come clothes, journeys, unexpected expenses like deaths, etc. The only way to get the cash needed is to become involved in the monetary sector.

CHANGING RELATIONS WITHIN THE HOUSEHOLD

I have said that wife and husband are independent production units, each cultivating different plots. The spouses are tied to each other through various claims on each other. The wife is responsible for cooking food, making beer, etc. She can sell beer and make mats to get an extra income for herself, thus strengthening her position as economically independent. A woman may make beer for sale about ten times a year, earning £S15–20 from it. The husband will give grain from his own cultivation to his wife (wives), and he should bring clothes from the market. He is also responsible for building and maintaining the house. He can earn additional incomes from the making of ropes and small beds (*engrib*) and the collecting of grass and branches to sell to people building houses.

The pattern of comsumption of a traditional household does not put great demands on the wife's time. During the day both sexes may be out drinking beer, or they may both be at the market place. If a guest comes, he/she will be brought to the place where beer is drunk to drink with the host. The only solid meal in the traditional Lafofa diet is dinner in the evening. This meal may consist of warm grain (*belila*) or the porridge (*asida*) with a sauce made of beans (*mullah lubia*). The wife is responsible for cooking and can make this meal in a couple of hours in the afternoon. Domestic duties make no great demand on the sexes, who have considerable time to be with other people, go to the market, etc.

This household pattern can still be observed, but younger households display a different pattern in which the wife is less active in productive work and in beermaking and, on the whole, is more confined to the house than is the case with older women. Many of the young men do not drink beer and do not frequent the beer-houses. While the old men and those among the young who do drink beer spend time at these gatherings, the non-drinkers may spend time in the market engaging in petty trade or visiting each other.

In households with people of this kind we can also observe a change in consumption patterns, modelled on the ordinary Sudanese household's customs. In these households, the consumption pattern is to have three meals a day, breakfast, lunch and dinner. If guests come, they should be treated to tea first and later to food. As they are guests of the house, it is important that they should stay there and eat. To make tea and food a wife is needed; and if three meals are to be prepared each day, there will not be much time to do other things. She would have to stay in or near the house in case guests should come.

Men who have been migrants together will visit each other and expect treatment like the one outlined. If a man is not able to fulfil these requirements, he will be scorned. In cases where people come to the house of a friend in which the wife is not present, the demand for tea will be extra strong and there will be jokes about the host not being a "man" since he cannot stop his wife from going out. Conflicts between the spouses were not uncommon after such events.

One important explanatory factor is the increasing cash needs that have affected the households. Such cash needs are related to the consumption patterns. As food requirements have changed, more things have to be brought from the market, like tea, coffee, sugar, etc. The availability of these things in the house, especially for treating guests, is a matter of prestige. Sugar is a case in point. Since sugar is rationed, people only get part of what they want from Government quotas, the rest they have to buy from traders at black market prices. Only people with cash can do this, and a common way for fellow villagers to express that a person has money is to say "he drinks sugar every day".

Requirements for clothes increased with Islam. People are expected to be decently dressed, and a family should have new clothes at the Islamic celebrations (*id al dahia, id ramadan*). Women want dresses, *taubes* and shoes, which has directly affected the demands women make of their men. They not only want clothes but also modern things for the house, like glasses, pots, and personal items like perfumes and mirrors.

The changing needs of the women are clearly displayed in their homes. Whereas a "traditional" woman will have a house with pots of various sizes hanging from the roof and standing on the floor, mats and beds for guests, small chairs, stoves for cooking, and tools for cultivation; the "modern" woman will have such things but also a table on which glasses, mirrors and bottles of perfumes are displayed. She will also have an iron box for keeping her dresses and *taubes*.

The needs of the women have changed. To fulfil these needs more cash is needed and the husband who is supposed to supply these things will have to bring in money. At the same time we have seen that women become less involved in income earning activities. They cultivate less and to an increasing extent stop making beer, because it is regarded as sinful in an Islamic context and shameful in a "Sudanese" context. The wife will, therefore, lose a source of income. These women still braid mats, but they cannot make up for this loss. They become increasingly dependent on their husbands to provide them with things. The relative status of the women is, therefore, greater dependence on the activities of the husbands.

The cash needs of the household are also affected by the changes in the socially necessary consumption. Public occasions like births and namegiving, circumcision, weddings and funerals were all occasions at which the traditionally major item of consumption used to be beer. Today, however, tea, sugar, coffee and oil are necessary for these occasions. Such occasions, being of social importance and necessary for the maintenance of a respected status in the village, further increase the significance of the husband's position since he is the one who earns the money to provide the necessities.

The need for cash within the household is, therefore, increasing and, as we have said several times, the opportunities to acquire money have changed as well. This has also implied a change in the relationships in which the Lafofa have been involved.

The cultivation of sorghum and peanuts on the mountain and sorghum and some cotton on far fields entailed contacts with *jellaba* traders and the Government officials dealing with the purchasing of cotton from the producers. As the majority of people were solely dependent on the mountain cultivation, and only during certain periods on far fields cultivation, we are justified in saying that in the traditional adaptation the opportunities to take part in income earning activities were equal for husband and wife. They could both cultivate food and grow cash crops like peanuts. The overall economic importance of this cultivation is, however, declining since it cannot satisfy the increasing needs for cash. With the growing importance of labour migration, Lafofa men have found a new possibility for earning money that is not available to their wives.

There is thus a general tendency among Lafofa households to require more cash to meet their increasing demands for consumption. This development has forced the men to bring in an extra income from outside the local village and migration to Khartoum has provided one such possibility. Since the men are now bringing in more cash, the wife is also more dependent on this cash. This, together with the impact of new values brought by the migrants as well as others, has brought about a change in the female role in Lafofa. We have seen how this manifests itself in a declining participation in beer making and cultivation and in an increasing degree of domestication. The general development of stronger ties between the spouses, leaving the man as the more powerful party, is also reflected in the development of divorces and the lack of ease with which women can get a divorce nowadays.

CHANGES IN ACCESS TO LAND AND LABOUR

Another factor that is important for the domestic unit is access to the production factors of land and labour. We have said in Chapter 3, that there is a difference in access to house fields and near fields on the mountain, compared to access to far fields on the plain. By clearing new land access to the latter is easy and far fields are thus not constrained by principles of land transfers in the same manner as on the mountain.

In this respect, the difference between Demri Gemr and the two brothers Kafi and Tia Ahmed is significant. Demri's father is an old man who has stopped farming and is only cultivating some square meters around his house. Demri has taken over his peanut plot which is one of the largest in the village. Ahmed, the father of Kafi and Tia, is, however, still active and cultivates all his land. They make up for this difference by cultivating far fields. My thesis, then, is that availability of land is not a constant constraint but will change with time and availability of opportunity.

Besides lack of land, the mobilization of labour is a constraint on the households. For far fields, the distance makes people reluctant to exploit them. People will not walk, work, and come back to the village to drink beer on the same day. People who do have some fields in the village can make use of the communal work parties. Their cost is, however, an important constraint. To mobilize a *hakuma* in 1979, £S6 was needed and this had risen to £S13 in 1981, due to inflation. To raise money for this a person would need to have a surplus of grain from the previous year. Young people do not cultivate a lot, so this possibility can be ruled out. The second possibility is to get money to buy all the things, which would mean continued labour migration.

We have now discussed the issue from the point of view of men. When we focus on women, the same explanation is valid for them. They get land from relatives or husbands and the availability of land may change over time. One important difference, however, is that women do not cultivate far fields or go on labour migration. Therefore, they do not have the same possibility as the men do to escape land shortage. The mobilization of labour is similar to that of the men and can be discussed in the same terms. But women have one important obligation that the men do not have. They make the beer for the work parties. Most young women are not experienced beer makers, and most of them attempt to make beer completely on their own for the first time after marriage. The skills of the new wife are, therefore, also a factor which limits the mobilization of labour and it affects both herself and her husband. Many of the migrant labourers are "good Muslims" who do not allow beer to be made in their houses. They cannot do wholly without beer if they want to mobilize other people and they therefore have to hire other women for this. We saw in our casestudies that Koshe, in Case 1, had her first try as a beer maker and also that Demri Gemr's wife did not make beer at all but that he had to hire other women to make beer.

5. Economic effects of adaptive choices

The focus of this chapter is an analysis of some implications for Lafofa household economies that arise from the different adaptive choices the household members make. The intention is to present an argument on how different variables are tied together to create and sustain the present economic forms in the area. We know that people are engaged in various economic activities; the major ones being cultivation, keeping animals, growing fruit-trees in orchards, doing wage labour and some trading. We have also seen how different units combine these activities to solve their problem of viability. We have seen that resources brought from outside the village itself are becoming more important. Paramount among these is wage labour. In Chapter 3 we have also seen how the socio-economic and cultural changes that the Lafofa are going through have also affected the ways in which Lafofa units solve their problems of adaptation.

In this chapter we shall see the effects of the various adaptational strategies and the new socio-economic and cultural rules on the units under discussion. The most significant trend is that some units, by making use of income from wage labour to increase their production locally, are able to strengthen their economic base. They do this by mobilizing labour in ways that are impossible for the poorer units. The various forms of collective labour, as well as hired labour, constitute a potential that can be mobilized by using the required skills and resources. All units do not possess the same level of skills and resources, which leads to some units being able to mobilize labour to increase production and others not.

A consequence of this development may be an increasing degree of differentiation among the village units. To what extent this will be the case and the extent to which such economic differences can be maintained depends largely on the investment possibilities outside agriculture. Such investment possibilities will be discussed with regard to the potential they represent as a basis for further economic differentiation among the Lafofa.

ECONOMIC PERFORMANCE

Building on our cases from Chapter 4, we may say that compared to young units the older ones are characterized by low needs. Both spouses are full producers, they have had a long time to solve the land problem, and the wife is an experienced beer maker. Compared to this, young couples have greater needs; only the husband is a full producer, they have a land problem, and the wife is an inexperienced beer maker or, due to Islamic influence, does not make beer at all. It remains to be seen, however, whether these factors create systematic differences in wealth between young and old households. To test this we shall look at the productive performance of our eight case units. The information is presented in Table 3.

From the table we see that the productive capacity of households cannot be used to explain differences in cultivation. As we see, the people who are able to and have the highest cost for mobilizing labour from *outside* the household also have the largest surplus. Labour power from outside the household, i.e. communal labour and wage labour, is, therefore, of crucial importance.

THE IMPORTANCE OF MOBILIZING LABOUR

To understand the implication of this it is necessary first to present information (Table 4) on the areas cultivated and the type of labour that has been used.

We see from the table that all possible types of labour are used, i.e. own labour, *nafir* (N), *hakuma* (H), *maliki* (M) and hired labour. We also see that the degree of use of hired labour or the collective labour institutions tends to increase with the size of cultivated plots. Labour should, therefore, be regarded as an investment that people can calculate on the basis of what they expect to get from the land and what they know to be the cost of the various types of labour. This is also confirmed by Table 5 which shows membership in and degree of mobilizing communal work groups.

Again we see that the unit doing the most cultivating on the mountain also mobilizes most labour. Since the *hakuma* and *maliki* can only be mobilized in turn, i.e. labour is exchanged reciprocally, it is only by mobilizing several *hakumas* and *malikis* that this labour potential can be exploited. We also notice that people engaged in far field cultivation do not have the option of using the communal work parties to help with their cultivation. They are thus dependent on relatives for help or on using hired labourers from the place where the far fields are situated. The Lafofa involved in far field cultivation are therefore affected by a regional labour market in a more direct way than their fellow tribesmen who concentrate their efforts on the mountain. On the mountain the different levels of production are not a result of differing productive capacity between the units but of their ability to mobilize labour from outside.

INCREASING COST OF LABOUR

Having seen how people actually make use of communal labour, we shall now look at how the cost of the different types of labour has developed. The high rate of inflation increases the cost of labour considerably.

Table 3.   *Subsistence needs and to which extent they are covered*

Units	Number of consumer (grown ups/children 0.5)	Total need for sorghum (kg per consumer/year: 240kg)	Total area of sorghum (m²)	Sorghum production (kg)	Total area of peanuts (m²)	Peanut production (sacks)	Value of peanut prod. (£S) (£S4/sack)	Peanut prod. converted into sorghum equivalents (kg)	Total production in sorghum equivalents (kg)	Size of surplus/deficit after consumption needs are covered (kg)	Size of surplus/deficit in money (£S) (1979 prices)	Cost of Labour (£S)	Net result (£S) (1979 prices)
Muhamed Koko	2.0	480	2,900	316	0	0	0	0	316	-164	-6.50	0	-6.50
Tia Ahmed	3.0	720	8,000	900	n.a.	n.a.	n.a.	n.a.	900	180	7.20	5*	2.20
Kafi Ahmed	2.0	480	24,000	1,800	n.a.	7	28	690	2,490	2,010	80.00	30*	50.00
Demri Gemr	5.0	1,200	3,000	328	11,200	28	112	2,660	2,988	1,788	76.00	47	29.00
Idris Enkato	4.5	1,080	4,500	493	3,700	8	32	760	1,253	174	7.00	16	-9.00
Jojo Omer	5.0	1,200	4,200	460	5,450	16	64	1,520	1,980	780	31.00	22	9.00
Umbelle Omer	5.0	1,200	5,000	548	n.a.	2	8	190	738	-460	-19.00	0	-19.00
Koko El Emin	2.0	480	4,700	515	920	4	16	380	895	415	16,50	8	8.50

* Freight cost to bring sacks to Liri

Table 4. *Size of plots (feddan) and type of labour used*

Producers	Area cultivated		Peanuts					Sorghum			
	pea-nuts	sorg-hum	sow	1st weed	2nd weed	3rd weed	clean-ing	sow	1st	2nd	har-vest
Muhamed	0	0.4						own	own	own	own
wife	0	0.4						own	own	own	own
Tia	n.a. (small)	4.5*	own	own	own	own	own	own	own/Br-own/Br/Fa		
wife	n.a. housef.							own	own	own	own
Kafi	n.a.	6*	own	own	own	own	own	own	own/hire –		own/Fa
wife	0	0									
Demri	2.8	0.6	hire	H	hire	hire	M	own	hire	N	own
wife	0	0.1	–	–	–	–	–	own	own	own	own
Idris	1.5	0.6	own	H	hire	own	N	own	own	own	own
wife 1	0.2	0.3	own	own	own	own	own	own	own	own	own
wife 2	0	0.1	–	–	–	–	–	own	own	own	own
Jojo	0.6	1.0	own	own	H	hire	own	own	hire	N	own
wife	0.7	0.3	own	hire	hire	N	own	own	hire	N	own
Umbelle	0.6	1.0	own	own	own	own	own	own	own	own	own
wife	0.8	0.3	own	own	own	own	own	own	own	own	own
Koko	0	0.9						own		own	own
wife	1.4	0.5	own	own	own	own	own	own	own	own	own

* far fields
measurement: 1 feddan = 1.04 acres or 0.42 hectare
Key: H – hakuma, M – maliki, N – nafir, hire – hired labour, own – own labour

This affects the traditional work parties most, since they involve the consumption of food items like grain, sugar, tea and beans, the prices of which are affected by this inflation. Wage labour does not show the same development. Wages do increase, but not at the speed of the other costs. Wage labour might be a favourable way of mobilizing labour, but the difficulty of getting enough people to work at the same time makes it problematic and wage labour has to be supplemented by the cooperative labour institutions. The inflation also underlines the importance of having a surplus from one's own production to use for this kind of investment, i.e. to avoid buying the grain at rising prices.

A second thing to note is the fact that the *nafir* that works only for beer is inexpensive compared to the one where the participants demand food (i.e. are Muslims). With the increasing involvement in Islam this might be an interesting trend affecting the development of the cost of labour.

The development of costs for a *hakuma* shows similar trends. To

Table 5. *Membership in and mobilization of work groups*

Units	Hakuma member	Hakuma mobilized	Maliki member	Maliki mobilized	Ordinary Nafir
Muhamed Koko	2	0	0	0	0
Tia Ahmed	1*	0	0	0	0
Kafi Ahmed	1*	0	0	0	0
Demri Gemr	3	3	1	1	1
Idris Enkato	1	0	0	0	0
Jojo Omer	1	1**	1	0	1
Umbelle Omer	0	0	1	0	0
Koko El Emin	1	0	1	0	0

  * *Hakuma* split because members did not want to work far fields
 ** *Hakuma* not mobilized for labour, but to put up money for Jojo to be used to
    hire labour

mobilize a *hakuma* a man will need about £S6 (1979) in cash. An example
of *hakuma* expenditure follows below

> 15 *midd* (45 kg) sorghum for beer, 5 *midd* (15 kg) for porridge, 30 pt. worth
> of milk for the porridge, worth of beans for the porridge, 11 pt. worth of
> red pepper, 10 pt. of salt and 5 pt. of onions.

These amounts are checked by other *hakuma* members; and if not provided, the person may be fined. The workers come on the day decided
upon and also have a strictly formalized work procedure. The formal ar-
rangement can be seen also in the amount of work that is supposed to be
done by each *hakuma* member. This is

> cleaning of peanuts: one man–one sack (=6 *safiha* à 16 l) = 20pt.

> weeding: one man–0.5 *Habil* (=250 m^2) = 20pt.

> fetch grass or branches from the mountain: one man–two loads/*ras* (what
> a man can carry on head) = 20pt.

Table 6.   *Comparison of cost of various types of labour (Pt.)*

| Type of labour | Cost per person | | Cost per *habil* (500m²) | |
	1979	1981	1979	1981
Nafir beer	5	18	42	150
food	10	27	83	225
Hakuma	22	56	44	112
Wage labour	25	50	40	80
grain price per *midd*	1979	17 Pt.		
	1981	60 Pt.		
sugar price per *rotl*	1979	25 Pt.		
	1981	50 Pt.		
tea price per *wagia*	1979	12 Pt.		
	1981	16 Pt.		
bean price per glass	1979	5 Pt.		
	1981	6 Pt.		

If one adds together the value of the labour in a *hakuma* (about 30 people), we see that the person arranging the work party gets £S6 worth of labour. Thus in 1979 there was a balance between what a man gives in food and what he gets back. With the inflationary development for the goods involved, an imbalance is developing between the cost in mobilizing a Hakuma and what one gets in return. In 1981 people were still claiming that the value of labour was the same (i.e. £S6), whereas the cost of mobilizing it had risen to £S13. The cost of local labour as it is perceived by people and arrived at through local bargaining does not increase at the same rate as inflation of the price of goods. The same is the case with the limited wage labour in the village. As wages are decided through bargaining, there is a smaller increase in wages than in prices for goods.

Table 6 confirms that the high rate of inflation increases the cost of labour considerably, which affects the traditional work parties most because they involve the consumption of food items like grain, sugar, tea, beans, etc. Wage labour does not show the same development. Wages increase, but not at the rate of the other items. Wage labour might be a favourable way of mobilizing labour, but it is hard to get enough people to work at the same time. The most effective labour groups are becoming rapidly more expensive, which will bring about sharper differentiation between those who can mobilize labour to increase production above household needs and those who cannot. We have said that Demri, i.e. the unit bringing in money from outside, is the one that can make best use of this communal labour. The mobilization of labour is crucial for success in local cultivation. Those who bring in money from outside can make use of it in order to increase cultivation. Wage labour is, therefore, more important than the internal capacity for production within the household. There is thus no systematic difference in the wealth of old as compared to young units, but rather between units of migrants as compared to non-migrants.

SOME IMPLICATIONS

From reciprocity to exploitation of labour

This development has several implications. First is the mobilization of labour itself. We have noted that the circulation of labour among households is governed by rules of reciprocity. People have equal opportunity to mobilize a work party, nobody can bypass the turn of the others. The person responsible for calling a *hakuma* or a *maliki* will be responsible for ensuring this. However, there are no rules against a person being a member of several parties, thus being able to mobilize several *hakumas* and *malikis*. We saw that Demri did this and that this strategy is dependent on his bringing in money from labour migration. Since he had access to good peanut land, it was a profitable strategy for him. This case shows an example not of reciprocity but of a *transfer* of labour from the "poor" to the "rich". With inflation making mobilization of labour more expensive, this will become more explicit. Since the cost of work groups is increasing more rapidly than that of wage labour, only the better off can afford this strategy, which in terms of labour mobilization is the most effective.

A case somewhat parallel to this is presented by Donham (1978, 1980) for the Malle of southwestern Ethiopia. In these communities there are three different types of formalized work groups, two reciprocal ones, *luhna* and *mol'o*, and one which is not reciprocal and can be mobilized as the means allow, *dabo*. The membership of this last group coincides with membership in two political factions. In faction A, which is led by traditional elders, labour is passed from the elders to the middle-aged. Donham argues that the logic behind this is the political domination of the elders which is maintained by their ability to sanction the youngsters by withdrawing their labour. In faction B, which contains wealthy immigrants, labour is systematically moving from the poor to the rich, showing that involvement in outside activities affects the mobilization of traditional labour groups.

Among the Lafofa, the mobilization of several work parties by one person indicates a similar trend. The constraint on this is access to land. Lack of land can easily be solved by the cultivation of far fields, but then the work parties are not available. However, the availability of wage labour on the plain is more plentiful and, as we have shown, its cost is less affected by inflation than communal labour, so that such a development may be beneficial to the units. Its implication for communal labour may well be that the *hakuma* and *maliki* will break down as institutions and that whatever tasks that need communal efforts will be done by ordinary work parties (*nafir*).

Although the principles for mobilizing labour are changing, communal labour can still be mobilized. But, as we have seen, the new ways of mobilization are more exposed to the inflationary development in the Sudanese economy. By bringing in money from wage labour one can still mobilize labour. The most crucial constraint on economic expansion in the village is that land cannot be monopolized, so there is a limit to the extent the work groups can be exploited.

Counteracting exploitation of traders

A second implication of the changing role of communal labour is seen in its function as saving clubs, thus acting as a way to counteract the need to enter into credit relationships with traders. In the Lafofa village there are three shops and, although they are small compared to those of the *jellaba*, the activities of the Lafofa traders also imply changing economic relationships. The largest of the traders, Muhamed, is constantly making small exchanges with the other Lafofa, buying things to resell to others or to bring them to other places to sell. An important aspect of this economic relationship within the village is that Muhamed is giving credit to the villagers, using the *shail* institution. Thus in July 1980 he gave people goods from his shop on credit. He gave each person goods worth of £S1.20 in return for a sack of peanuts. 20 people traded 40 sacks of their future peanut harvest in this manner. In February the following year Muhamed could sell peanuts to the local jellaba at £S7 a sack. The appearance of Lafofa traders has thus also resulted in new credit relationships being introduced in the village. The volume of these transactions is small, but it is socially significant, as it adds to the general process of commercialization and the new forms of socio-economic inequality.

One traditional way to counteract the need for people to engage in credit relationships has been to use the *hakuma* and *maliki* as saving clubs. I observed one *hakuma* which had £S120 in its box. In June 1981, which is the time for hard labour and a regular food intake is needed, the members decided to take out £S4 each so that they did not have to borrow from the local traders, whether Lafofa or *jellaba*. After the harvest they agreed to bring back one sack of peanuts each to the *hakuma* to be sold. Nobody was allowed to pay the £S4 in cash. If they did not grow peanuts, they would have to buy a sack. At the time the deal was done, a sack of peanuts was worth about £S10 on the local market. With inflation the sum would increase and so would the money in the box, which could be used as common capital again. Other *hakumas* have less money and the members cannot get this kind of help. In any case, as developments seem to reduce the importance of communal work groups, no organizational framework for this kind of self help will remain and people will be more directly forced into entering credit relationships with traders.

ALTERNATIVE INVESTMENT OPPORTUNITIES

We shall now turn to the other investment opportunities that are found on the mountain to see what implications they have.

Focusing on performance in cultivation is only part of the story. The adaptation of a Lafofa household is dependent on the total range of resources at the unit's disposal and its adaptive strategy will be formed as a result of the management of a totality of resources. We shall, therefore, see how people go about making investments and also how they "cover" apparent deficits in their cultivation (Table 7).

We see that those with a deficit make use of the option presented by the Baida scheme to earn money. The willingness of the Lafofa to go to the scheme thus seems dependent on their economic situation, and it appears that they go there to earn a "target-income", i.e. to earn money for specific reasons. An interesting exception to this is Umbelle Omer who has enough cattle to sell off an ox to cover a deficit. Although he appears in the table with the biggest deficit and has also withdrawn from his *hakuma*, people talked about him as being well-off, always referring to his cattle.

We cannot, therefore, draw conclusions on the basis of cultivation alone, who is well-off, but should look at the totality of resources.

As for the units that make investments, they do most of the cultivating as well as bringing incomes from outside. We have seen that investments in labour are a major factor in this. We have, however, not discussed the other investment targets and what implications they have for the differentiation process. The two most significant are trade and animals.

The type of trade open to the Lafofa is petty trade, selling mats, fruits, cigarettes, cloth, etc. The market is crowded with people doing the same thing and the possibilities for expansion are limited. Another trading alternative is to open a shop. Obviously there is not room for many more shops in the village, as there are three there already. The shops and the involvement of the Lafofa in trade are important to the local community in several ways, as they entail changing economic relationships.

A final investment possibility for the mountain Lafofa is the various animals they may acquire. Although the surpluses in the Lafofa economy

Table 7.   *Investment of surplus and covering of deficit*

Units	Investment			Cover Deficit	
	Animals bought	Second wife	Shop	Animals sold	Trips to al Baida
Muh. Koko	0	0	0	0	2
Tia Ahmed	0	0	1	0	0
Kafi Ahmed	6 goats	0	0	0	0
Demri Gemr	1 cow (30%)	1	0	0	0
Idris Enkato	0	0	0	0	2
Jojo Omer	1 goat	0	0	0	0
Umbelle Omer	0	0	0	1 ox	0
Koko El Emin	0	0	0	1 ox	0

are not large enough to start a rapid growth of the herds through investments, the possibility is still there; and people do make use of it. But there
are also other constraints on the success of this strategy. In the mountain
herd female animals are more easily lost through accidents than in the
lowland. Animals are valuable to the Lafofa as they increase the
threshold of economic security. They also help improve the family's diet
especially by providing small children with milk. They also affect the labour allocation within the family since they are also herded during cultivation. Partnerships can come about both by two people sharing an animal, or through plains residents sending their herds up to the mountain
during harvesttime on the far fields.

LIMITS TO ECONOMIC GROWTH

In the discussion in this chapter I have concentrated on how the Lafofa
units have managed to keep themselves viable as socio-economic units
and what types of constraints they met. The important ones were access
to land and the mobilization of labour. I also argued that access to production factors became a smaller problem over time, because more land
could become available and experience in cultivation and in mobilizing
labour was increasing. For the units which managed to create a surplus,
there remained the problem of how to invest it. One obvious possibility
would be to invest it in the production factors themselves, in order to
create a "spiral of growth". In the following I shall discuss this possibility
as well as others to identify the opportunities for and the limits to economic growth which the Lafofa face.

Land: I have not come across cases of land sales. A person will, therefore, have to follow the traditional ways of getting land. On the mountain

we saw that the complex procedure of getting land from different relatives and at different times provides an effective limit on the accumulation of land. The far fields are different. As long as land is not scarce in an area, one can increase one's acreage, thereby monopolizing it for oneself. We have seen that distance and availability of labour are the main limits for the Lafofa in their cultivation of far fields.

Labour: On the mountain labour is mobilized mainly through beer parties, although hired labour is also important. Surpluses can be invested in more labour. But expansion on the mountain is limited by the lack of land and the fact that all the people mobilized for labour are themselves independent producers who will not enter into long-term agreements on labour. In the far fields, wage labour could be used more extensively, since there are poor people travelling around looking for work. But the Lafofa would be competing for this labour power on a regional labour market where large farmers, traders, etc. are operating.

Technology: Hoe cultivation is limited in terms of possible technological investments. One might join a scheme to get access to the mechanical equipment (NMAPC-schemes) and some Lafofa do have small plots there. But at the current price developments the cultivation of cotton is not profitable. For farmers to mechanize on their own would require credit from outside. Such credit does exist, but is channelled to the merchants.

Petty trade: Marketing one's surplus and investing the money in goods like mats, fruits, cigarettes, cloth, etc. to resell at a different market may also bring some money and it may be worthwhile for an individual to do this. But each market is crowded with people doing the same thing. To establish a shop in the mountain village is possible, but would need more surplus than can be earned in one year. There are now three shops already, so there is hardly room for more. It thus seems to be checks on the possibilities for expansion within the trade sector. The new opportunities provided by the withdrawal of the *jellaba* from the consumer trade to concentrate on mechanized farming (described in Chapter 1) are a significant factor affecting developments in Liri. This opening up of trade has provided the Lafofa and other groups with possibilities that were not there before and which are not present in many other places in the Nuba Mountains.

Orchards: What was said about orchards in Chapter 4 indicates that people try to establish them and, once established, they bring no insignificant profit. One informant told me that in one year he earned £S7 from one mango tree in his garden. Furthermore he got £S10 from six guava trees and £S3 from two lemon trees. This is an income of £S20 from a small garden. But planting an orchard requires much effort during the first years, both in watering the trees and fencing to keep out animals. The fact that the young men go away on labour migration means that they cannot look after their trees. Some have managed, however, and on the whole the establishment of orchards seems to be on the increase among the Lafofa. Such an establishment is, of course, independent of the size of surplus from production, and anyone can do it. They offer, therefore, no immediate solution to the problem of where a surplus could be channelled.

Animals: Animals are the most common investment object on the savanna, which is also the case among the Lafofa. Yet the size of the surplus is not large enough to initiate rapid growth in a herd of cattle. No one in the mountain had acquired a number of cattle large enough to provide the basis for existence, though they remain an important security object. In principle, animals will be a possible investment target; and the Lafofa living on the plains, having a larger production due to their more extensive cultivation of far fields, may invest in more animals.

We have now seen the ways in which the Lafofa tried to make themselves viable in their ecological and socio-economic environment. To stay viable they made use of their own traditional agricultural sector and took part in the monetary system through cash crop cultivation and labour migration. Some managed to create a small surplus which could be invested productively and became basis for economic growth. Yet we have also seen the effective checks on investment. Cattle remained a general investment object, but given the ecological environment, there is a high risk of loss of animals. Even if one is successful, by accumulating more animals one would have to leave the mountain. The mountain village would, therefore, not experience a spiral of growth based on its traditional adaptation to cultivation and animal husbandry.

The Lafofan economy is stagnant, only maintaining itself through inputs from outside. This comes as no surprise and the Lafofa fit into the general pattern we have seen elsewhere on the savanna. However, there are investment possibilities in trade, and surpluses may be put into that sector. One implication of such a strategy is that in doing so the Lafofa develop closer links with the regional market populations in Liri.

This development of integration and involvement in the market sector does not change the fact that the Lafofa is a marginal group in Liri, economically as well as socially; but the pursuit of such strategies does have profound effects on the Lafofa themselves. We shall now turn to a discussion of such effects.

6. Participating in a plural region: Some implications

We shall now return to the plurality of the Liri region and see how the developments in integration have effected the Lafofa as a social and cultural group. We have said that the Nuba are leaving their intensive cultivation system, are moving from their mountain village to settle on the plains and are involved in the cultivation of cash crops. They are also involved in labour migration to various regional towns and to Khartoum. We have also seen some of the implications of such activities at the economic level. In this chapter I shall deal primarily with yet another level: how these developments affect the Lafofan culture and way of life. The discussion is meant to show how cultural expressions are integrated with other aspects of the Lafofas' lives and how we have to look at this as a whole way of life in order to understand how new cultural idioms are created and derive their meaning.

MAJOR THEMES DEFINING PLURALITY IN LIRI

The population of Liri is composed of a number of different ethnic groups, each representing a distinct cultural heritage. Such a cultural heritage is defined by factors like origin, language, dress and a distinct kinship network (Barth, 1983:37). Not all of these factors are of equal importance in Liri, and in the following I shall point out some of the major features that help distinguish the Lafofa from the Arab groups.

Languages

One important difference between the Lafofa and the Arabs is the language difference. Although Arabic is established as a lingua franca and most Nuba speak Arabic, the existence of distinct Nuba languages is an important factor confirming the identities of the various Nuba groups. One characteristic of the Nuba Mountains is the existence of a multiplicity of languages and dialects. In Liri the three Nuba groups living in close proximity to each other speak three distinct languages. Liri is a sub-language of the larger Talodi-Mesakin language group. Similarly, Talasa is part of the Kadugli-Korongo language. Lafofa makes up a language group of its own, together with the small Amira group, people who live just south of Liri. Quoting the 1956 National Population Census of Sudan, Stevenson (1984:28) puts the number of Lafofa speaking people

Table 8.   *Arab descent groups as exemplified by one Hawazma section*

Main section	Section	Minimal section
		Dar Bakhoti
	Dar Gawad	Dar Shalongo
Abd el Ali	Awlad	
	Ghabosh	Dar Batha
		Awlad Ba'ashom
		Dar Debl
		El Ma'anat
		Awlad Gama'a
	Dar Betti	Awlad abu Adam
		El Kura'an
	Dar Na'ayli	

at 5,140 (see MacDiarmid & MacDiarmid, 1931; and Stevenson, 1956, 1962, 1964 for linguistic characteristics of Lafofa and other Nuba languages).

Descent systems

The Lafofa belong to the matrilineal belt of the Nuba Mountains. This matrilineality is expressed in a descent ideology that regards the descendants in the mother's line as a unilineal group and membership of that group is transferred through women. In contrast to the Arabic system, a child does not belong to the descent group of its father but to that of its mother. Furthermore, there are no named descent groups.

The implication of this for children is that they stay with their mother, even in the case of divorce. The relationship between a MoBr and SiSo is also important. It is emphasized by the kin terminology in which a single term is used for the two (*imbing*).

The people of Liri who are called "Arabs" are of either the *Hawazma* or the *Kawahla* groups. They belong to a descent structure that is common to most Arabs in the Sudan and that is characterized by patrilineal descent with named sections and sub-sections. The *jellaba* consist of people of Arab as well as Nubian origin. In the context of descent, their systems would be similar to that presented below.

Using the Hawazma as an example, the picture is shown in Table 8.

The basic solidarity within this system is between men, and relationships between father and son and between brothers are important. For organizational purposes, the descent groups can be mobilized and will act together against outsiders. This system resembles Evans-Prichard's *segmentary system*.

Kin-terms

Another important feature distinguishing the kinship system of the Arabs from that of the Nuba is that of kin-terms.

What Figure 8 shows is two distinctly different systems. The Arabs use different terms to distinguish between both *sex* and *generation*. The Lafofa system is a classificatory system using the same terms for brother and sister in the ego's generation, and for siblings on the father's side. We see that on the mother's side, the mother's brother is singled out with a term different from that of mother's sister. This reflects the matrilineal kinship system and the important relationship between a boy and his MoBr. We shall see later what implications this distinction has for the Lafofa as they operate in non-Lafofa settings. For our descriptive purpose here, the above presentation is sufficient.

Concepts of inferiority and superiority

Religious adherence

Although today most people in Liri would claim to be Muslims, it is still important to focus on the basic difference between being a Muslim and a non-Muslim. For identity purposes this is also a distinction that divides the Nuba (as non-Muslims) from the Arabs as Muslims. The picture is, however, more complicated than this. Looking at individual cases shows that there is a process of Islamization going on and that the Nuba are leaving their traditional religious beliefs and practices.

More secondary distinctions in the area are those between the *sufi*-orders and the mosque, representing the basic Islamic distinction between the *umma* and the *sufi*. And there is the distinction between the various *sufi*-sects, the dominant one in Liri being the Qadiriyya, but the Tijaniyya is also represented, especially among the *fellata*.

The "slave–freeman" (abid–hurr) distinction

The history of the Nuba Mountains is that of a frontier. It was a field of economic and human exploitation and an arena where ethnic and societal transformations took place (O'Fahey, 1982). One important source of a stigmatised status was that of slave origin. In the Sudan the sterotype of the Nuba and other frontier populations is partly that of belonging to an enslaved population. In the wider system of social stratification the slave–freeman distinction follows the Nuba–Arab distinction.

Figure 8. *Lafofa and Arab kin-terms compared*
(see also Fig. 4)

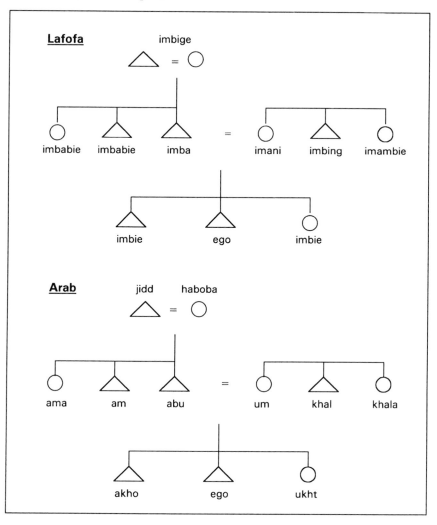

In Liri, however, this distinction is applied in a different way. It is related to the fact that all Nuba in Liri had not been enslaved. Being in the
very south of the Nuba Mountains the populations in Liri were those
which managed to run away from enslavement. Some groups did have a
past as slaves. They are some of the people who to-day claim Hawazma
and Kawahla descent. They are descendants of actual, run-away slaves,

and have taken on an assimilated identity. This identity is accepted as Arab in everyday life; but, as we saw in Chapter 1, it becomes important in certain contexts within the field of local politics.

PLURALITY AS PART OF AN INTERACTIONAL GAME

The languages, descent systems, kin-terms and identities such as Muslim–non-Muslim and slave–freeman are clearly important identity markers for the Liri people. There may be others as well and we cannot explain all differences that are of relevance for such participation. Rather we should look at the total plural situation, not in order to demarcate cultural boundaries between the groups, but to see in what way members of such groups participate in the plural situation (Barth, 1982). Through such participation, people activate certain parts of their cultural background in interaction; and they choose to participate in specific ways, thus embracing certain identities to the exclusion of others. Members of the same group, i.e. with fairly similar cultural backgrounds, can pursue different strategies of identity management and make use of different parts of their cultural inventory to emphasize who they are. Participating in such a plural situation is also a source of learning for the participants, whom one may follow in other situations, to see to what extent they take on or embrace new traits. To show this I shall focus on the participation of different groups of Lafofa as they appear on some arenas in Liri.

HOW THE LAFOFA PARTICIPATE IN THE PLURAL REGION

With these qualifications of the Liri region as an arena for interaction, let us proceed to some examples of how the Lafofa actually behave on that scene. I have chosen the market place and the local court as examples, because they are arenas in which the Lafofa are most explicitly exposed to the plural situation. The people involved are all Lafofa still living in the mountain village. Through the examples I want to show how the cultural characteristics described not only operate as identity markers but also as qualities that the people involved bring with them when they want to interact on this regional arena.

The market place

As a market center the Liri market town, Tunguru, is similar to any market place in the Sudan. A square surrounded by shops and warehouses, with vegetables, fruit and meat being sold within the market area. This inner *suq* is dominated by the shop-owners, the *jellaba*, who spend their days sitting under the trees, seemingly idle, but running their shops and lorries from there. Outside the main *suq* are some trees where petty trade goes on. One of these is the place where most Lafofa come when they have something to sell. Now, if we, for instance, go back up the mountain and start from there one early morning, we will see people leave their houses to walk down to the market. Some of them will be in ordinary clothes, carrying wood or grass on their heads, intending to sell this at the market. They will start on their journey and if we walk with them, we will probably stop at a house where beer is for sale and spend an hour there drinking. We will then proceed to descend the mountain and stop at its foot before entering the market. The Lafofa will dry his sweat, put on more decent clothes and place his load behind some rock near the path. He will then go into the market and ask some traders in Arabic if they need what he brought. He may sell it to anyone, being told to bring it to a trader's house and come back for money. When the Lafofa gets his money, he will disappear from the market place, go to the village where he knows people, and drink beer. He will spend the day there, only to return in the afternoon before sunset.

Compare this to a young migrant, who leaves his house wearing nice trousers and a shirt bought in Khartoum. He will not be carrying anything, but will go directly to a friend's house down on the plain to fetch the grain, cigarettes, dates, etc. that he left there the day before. He will bring this to the "Lafofa tree," sit down, and act as a trader. As more Lafofa boys come, he will ask someone to look after his boxes and will himself walk around the market to look for friends. Maybe they will have tea, maybe they will watch the *jellaba* as they play their games and listen to their conversation about trade matters. Their whole interaction will be conducted in Arabic, and they will look like most other young boys at the market.

Both groups of Lafofa are marginal at the market, economically as well as socially. They have to adapt to the established code of the market and act accordingly. But while the first one only makes use of the market to earn the money he needs and then withdraws to more familiar contexts, the migrant spends all his day in the market-place in a much more exposed way and has to act in a way that is acceptable in this context. That this difference is also registered by other actors in the market is clearly shown by the different ways of talking about them. For the first type of Lafofa negative stereotypes are used like, "they do not have any religion, the *marissa*-people", etc.; whereas for instance, when the migrants appeared at the market after having returned from Khartoum, they were talked about as "the mountain boys are becoming OK, they pray, they work hard, they are moving forwards".

The local court

My second example is taken from the local court, the *mahkama*, in Liri. This local, customary court makes up one branch of the pluralistic judicial system in the Sudan. There are two major hierarchies of courts, the *Sharia Division* and the *Civil Division* (see Jalil, 1984). The former administers Islamic law as it relates to personal status, mainly family law. For the Liri region the *Sharia* court with responsibility for that area is in Rashad. The judge (*qadi*) comes to Liri once a year to deal with cases of divorce, etc. The Civil Division administers the European type law introduced by the British. At the lower end of this hierarchy are the customary courts. Although they have their restrictions on what cases they can deal with, these courts pass judgement mainly according to customary tradition. With the ethnic heterogeneity of the Sudan this means that any generalization is impossible. Their importance is undisputed and in 1975, for example, it was assessed that about 70 per cent of the judicial work in the Sudan was undertaken by such courts (Jalil, op.cit.:2).

Through such dispute settlements, the courts advocate certain ideologies and values and are thus foci of ideology influencing local areas. In a "frontier region" like Liri, with its complex population of Arabs–non-Arabs, Muslims–non-Muslims, the court, with its basis in Arabic culture and Islamic religion, must act as an important agent of change. Local people are "taught" how to act properly before the court, e.g. in cases involving disputes between spouses, drinking, public behaviour, etc. The court is also a place where people, like the Lafofa, can take their conflicts when they cannot or do not want to solve them through their local *sheikh*, or a local committee (*lejna*), as is also commonly done. I shall not go into detail about all types of cases that appear before the court, but try to outline some of the *style of rhetoric* that is found there.

When a person presents his case at such a local court he will start with the initial Islamic "*b'ism'Allahi*" and then go on to present his story. The presentation always takes a long time, many issues are mentioned, some highly relevant, others less so. But in all cases the presentations are rich in details and examples of events that can present the speaker in a favourable light, stressing generosity, manliness and other basic Sudanese values. This rhetorical style is approved by the audience which sits in a semi-circle in front of the court. As in any court room, I suppose, a clear argument which makes others, be they judge or audience, accept a certain interpretation of the case, is the issue that is at stake here. The presentations are thus in a way negotiations in which one's identity and honor is at stake. Therefore, many cases end in quarrels as one makes accusations about other people, who immediately respond (see e.g. Geertz, 1983 and Grønhaug, 1984 for discussions of similar aspects).

I have made the above presentation in order to make the reader see the context a Lafofa enters when he enters a local court. His Arabic is not without flaws, his command of the rhetorical skills even more limited. The *mahkama* is thus an arena where the position of the Lafofa in relation to the wider society is clearly signalled. But still some Lafofa make use of this court and, as they do that, we can see how being Lafofa affects their performance in court and how they argue around this. A few cases will illustrate these points.

Case 1

The village trader, Mohamed, has reported his sister's husband to the court for not buying a *taube* for her. Furthermore, the sister is pregnant but she does not receive money or food from her husband. The husband is also related to Mohamed. In his presentation of the case, Mohamed refers to the way women should be treated by their husbands and also makes a point of the husband in this case letting his sister go about "naked". Can I, as a brother, look at that without taking any action? asks Mohamed. What will people say if a man leaves his wife naked? It is not right! The husband of Mohamed's sister is not in the court, but a brother has come, to tell the *mahkama* that his brother is an ignorant man and has just refused to come to court. He is also very poor.

The court's decision is clear. A man is responsible for clothing his wife. If there is no money then he should borrow some from his brothers. A *taube* should be provided and should be bought before the next *mahkama*. In the next court the same people appear, the husband's brother bringing an inexpensive *taube*. Mohamed makes fun of the quality, calling it "a poor man's *taube*". But he accepts it and asks about the money for food. The brother of the accused can only report that his brother has refused to pay, saying he has no money. "At least he has the money for *marissa*", Mohamed says, but is stopped by the court president, as it is not his turn to speak.

The court decides that the parties involved should make up a committee (*lejna*) and that this committee should decide on how much should be paid. The court leaves no doubt about the fact that something should be paid. A man is responsible for his wife, especially when she is pregnant with his child.

What is expressed here is first, that a local trader is making use of the court to protect the interests of his sister. He is appealing to the Sudanese concept of how a woman should be treated, arguing that going without a *taube* is equal to being naked. Mohamed's is an interesting case, because he is the first trader to have established a shop in the village and has assimilated Sudanized language use, dress and general appearance in public.

Case 2

The second case is between a husband and one of his two wives. The man has brought his wife to court for not having prepared food for him, not looking after the children, and not making a mat (*birish*) for him. She refuses to do all this in spite of the fact that he gives her money. She never buys anything for this money but gives it to her mother instead. The wife is there in the court and maintains that she never gets anything from her husband. Even when she accompanied him to al Fawa, the cotton scheme, to work, she did not get her fair share of the income.

The court decides that the husband shall give his wife money. She is his second wife, and the court warns him against favouring one wife over the other, referring to the Koran where it is clearly stated that a man shall only take a second wife if he is able to treat both fairly. The wife is told to give her husband a mat to sleep on if he is entitled to that, and to look after her house. The husband takes to the floor after the *mahkama* is over and tries to tell how he sees the relations between spouses. He is a Muslim and knows these things well, he claims. The court and the audience laugh, and the court-president tells him not to waste their time but go straight to the market and have the wife's dress made.

Several things can be elaborated here. As in the first case, it shows what is supposed to be the reciprocal responsibility of the spouses and the court teaches and judges at the same time. As the man has two wives, the problem of equality between the wives is also raised and stressed. The end of the case, where the husband tries to compensate for his defeat in the case by trying to reestablish his position by showing he commands Islamic ideas about marriage, shows that his claims are not appreciated by the audience or the court. It clearly demonstrated how little the court thinks of the Lafofa knowledge and status in these matters.

Let me end these examples from the court by focusing on a different way in which traditional Lafofa notions become exposed as being marginal in such a plural situation. This relates to a case involving a land dispute. Let me begin with the case itself.

Case 3

A Lafofa man, Demri, has brought a woman to court, accusing her of cultivating a plot that he claims to be his, passed to him from his grandfather and then his father, who had died the year before. Demri starts explaining his case and does this in the normal way by establishing the relationships from which he claims his right.

The case gets complicated when the woman also claims to have links to the grandfather of Demri. Demri explains how that relation is, saying that she was allowed to cultivate by a man related to his grandfather. Demri systematically refers to this man as his father's MoBrDa (*bint khal'uh*). The men at the court shake their heads, and the vice-president of the court calls upon the court assistant, a Lafofa man, to "translate". There is a time of joking and head-shaking, while people talk about the mountain people and the way they reckon descent through women. "It is no system", they say.

The president of the court says the *mahkama* cannot accept concepts about mother-rights, but it wants to have the terms translated into words they can understand. The court assistant is also unable to explain these terms and the case is solved by the court sending the parties involved to an old man living nearby. He is a Lafofa who will remember the relationships. They should clear up their differences there, with the old man.

What is at stake here is the right to land. The important point is not the verdict as such, although we should note the court's willingness to have a case settled according to the Lafofa way of thinking. The *mahkama* clearly in this case, as in many others, accepts the pluralistic context in which it works. But more important here is Demri's inability to explain the relationship that he thought was proof that he had a right to the land. To the court and the audience his mixing of sexual terms while talking about men was funny and emphasized that the Lafofa are different. A quick glance at the indigenous Lafofa kin-terms (Figures 4 and 8) will however reveal the problem Demri had. In their kin-term system the Lafofa do not discriminate between brother and sister within the same generation. A brother and a sister are called by the same name, *imbie*, among the Lafofa. In Arabic usage one discriminates between the two, i.e. *akho, ukht*. In a court case, a Lafofa's inability to translate these terms into terms that are meaningful to the court may limit his/her ability to express the real content of his/her thoughts.

Although ethnic identities are not directly relevant for market transactions and court proceedings, the culture of the participants in these settings is not irrelevant for the interaction which evolves. In the above three cases, we have seen how participating in these settings presents the Lafofa with opportunities and constraints which favoured the adoption of cultural features from their neighbours and made it difficult to communicate their own identity.

We have also seen the variation in people's participation, with the migrants participating and exposing themselves more to the dominant ideas about acceptable behaviour and conduct on the Liri scene. The old-timers are also able to operate on that scene. They speak Arabic and know enough to get their business done. An important point is to determine whether the difference is that their adaptation is merely a "role-switch," whereas the migrants "embrace" the values and standards of the plural scene and also make them relevant to their lives in the mountains. An important next step is therefore to see to what extent this interaction in the plural region also leads to changes on the mountain, because the migrants do new things there as a consequence of their adaptive strategies and new identity management.

THE CHANGING MEANING OF SIGNS

We have seen that the Lafofa labour migrants are more inclined to acquire an Islamic identity and to adopt Arabic customs than were the old-timers. The wives of such migrants show similar characteristics when compared to the elder women. We have also seen that the migrants stand out in their willingness to make use of regional arenas in which they are exposed to the ways of other groups and that they make efforts to adapt to these customs in the way they present themselves and interact. In this section I want to ask the important question about how we can establish the links between the interactional intercourse the Lafofa are involved in within a wider region and the elements of change observed on the mountain. That is, what are the effects of new economic strategies on local culture and how can we link processes on an economic level to those on a cultural level? A major question to be answered is whether there are empirical relations between the creation of specific symbols and activities in the economic field. Signs are not arbitrary, but are more or less useful in assisting someone to fit into a certain code. My specific interest is in those signs that are not only signs, but which at the same time have implications for productive life, division of labour, etc. Thus one major task is to show how the economic participation of the Lafofa in labour migration, local cultivation and other activities has brought about changes in the signs that are bound up with the same activities. To start this discussion I shall use aspects of local cultivation and labour mobilization among the Lafofa, because this is one field in which I believe such inter-relationships can be established.

LOCAL CULTIVATION AND LABOUR MOBILIZATION

We saw in the economic discussion in Chapters 4 and 5 how Lafofa migrants, by bringing in money from their migration, managed to do new things in local cultivation, particularly in the field of mobilizing labour. This was particularly effective because the Lafofa have several types of work groups, not only the *nafir*, but also the more formalized *hakuma* and *maliki*. The economic effect of this was to change reciprocal labour institutions into institutions that could bring about economic differentiation. Literature on labour mobilization and communal work groups, in particular, has already shown that such labour mobilization is not only an economic matter related to production but that it is also closely related to socio-cultural elements of society. This is true of the work parties themselves (Abrahams, 1965; Barth, 1967 a,b; Gulliver, 1971; O'Laughlin, 1973; Charsley, 1976) and of the beer, the most important item of reward in African communal labour (Sangree, 1962; Netting, 1964; Hutchinson, 1979). It is to such broader fields of Lafofa labour organization that we

shall now turn, relating some recent changes in the use of communal labour and beer to important processes of change within Lafofa society. My
main example will be taken from the *hakuma*. A general description of
various types of labour institutions was given in Chapters 2 and 3, and in
Chapter 5 I showed the economic role that they play. Here I shall concentrate on the ways in which a *hakuma* is organized as a ritual organization.

The Hakuma

A Hakuma Gathering: the annual meeting

In preparation for this particular annual party an ox had been bought to
be slaughtered. The price was £S45 and the members collected £S20
among themselves and were to pay the rest later. Every member paid 25
piasters directly, the rest was taken from the money box. In addition, every
member brought 1 *midd* (about 3 kg) of sorghum, plus 6 piastres for the
mill. When the ox was slaughtered, every member collected some meat and
brought it home for his wives to prepare.

The wives also made beer and porridge from the sorghum. When the
women had finished their work, they brought the food to the place where
the party was being held, under a big tree, near the house of the leader of
this particular *Hakuma*. Outside the house, where the women sit, a place
had been prepared with some areas fenced in and a flag posted at the entrance. The physical layout of the place is presented in Figure 9.

The person responsible for food and beer came before the others to
check that all the required things were there. Another person was responsible for letting people in, and would also come early. When people started
coming they stopped at a white flag that signaled the entrance and waited
for this person. He asked them for their "grade", according to which they
would be shown where to sit in. There were five different places to sit.
When people who were not members of this *Hakuma* came, they went
through the same procedure. The most "important" people sat in squares
II and III on Figure 9, areas fenced in by thin poles marking them off from
the others. Anyone wanting to enter either of these places had to consult a
soldier first. He was standing guard by the flag outside square II which is
the *Mudiria*, or Government Headquarters. Any request ought to be in
writing, which for obvious reasons was not possible, so it was done orally.

If a complaint was raised about bad behaviour, unnecessary noise, cheating to get extra beer, etc., one addressed the *Mudir*, the leader of the
Mudiria, who would come out to settle the matter. These discussions always
took a long time, threats of fining each other and references to *Hakuma*-
rules would go back and forth and normally everything would be settled
without anyone being fined.

The soldier had a whistle. When he blew it three times, everyone was
supposed to be silent. This would be done when they distribute beer, give
messages or to count money. The silence is to help those who distribute
beer or count money to concentrate, so that justice can be done. These oc-

casions are impressive, especially at the beginning; but after beer drinking has gone on for some time, cheating starts and many disputes develop.

All members of the *Hakuma* are well dressed at these occasions. No half-naked bodies would be seen, as would be the case on any other day in the village. To dress in a bad way would be to insult the *Hakuma* and a fine would have to be paid. At these ceremonies new members would join the *Hakuma*. The new members would enter the *Mudiria* and be given their ranks. When all new members have theirs, the soldier would blow his whistle three times two, and people would clap their hands and congratulate the newcomers.

As I said, the ranks were grouped together so that all equals would be together. There were four different groups, with the *Mudiria* (II) and *Zeriba al Malik* (III) on top. These were fenced in, and there would be beds to sit on. The other two groups had to bring their own chairs or used logs that they found. These were the *Dobbat* (officers) and the *Khabat* (the forestry department). Finally there were the *Arabs*, i.e. those persons who do not belong to any *Hakuma*. They would sit some distance away from the others, clearly marked off as outsiders.

All ranks are temporary, in the sense that they cannot be taken outside the context of the *Hakuma* gathering and made to apply in everyday life. But when the *Hakuma* has a meeting, they are positions everyone accept.

I have described the annual party when new members are brought into the *hakuma*. This occasion is more elaborate and on a larger scale than the ordinary meetings after work has been done for any of the members. Although the fencing is not there, the groups keep apart; and *hakuma*-life is played out in basically the same way.

Changing principles of mobilization

An important aspect of communal labour is the way in which it can be mobilized. For the ordinary *nafir*, the people working together are asked to come by the person arranging the work. They are relatives, in-laws, neighbours and others who may include passers-by and who decide to work for some beer. In the more formalized parties, the *hakuma* and *maliki*, it is mainly one's place of residence which will decide which group one belongs to. There are *hakumas* and *malikis* from different parts of the village, which are called by the names of their areas. There is a *hakuma teht* (down under) which is from the western part of the village, an area which slopes down the ascending plain to the western market. There is also the *hakuma Lotiro* in the northern part of the village, called Lotiro.

There are exceptions to this pattern of membership. One factor is the fact that the Lafofa are now spread out, and a man may have fields in the mountain village as well as on the plains. The same goes for a man living on the plains but still cultivating a field in the mountain. Such a person will join the *hakuma* at the place where his field is. Secondly non-Lafofa

Figure 9. *Spatial lay-out of a hakuma gathering*

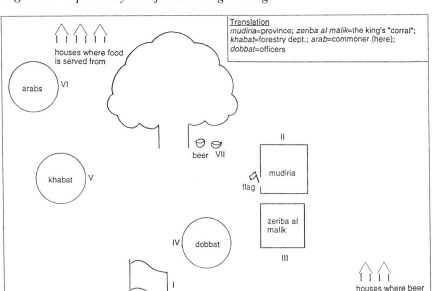

can now become members of the *hakuma*. The two largest cultivators
from Liri, the second mountain village still inhabited in the area, are both
members of a Lafofa *hakuma*. Thirdly, the Islamized Lafofa, who do not
drink beer, have their own *hakuma*. The general process of Islamization
and the appearance of new life styles among the Lafofa is thus bringing
about new recruitment patterns for communal work groups. Religious
identity and attitudes toward beer now determine membership.

Changing ritual practices

The migrants organize their own communal work group where no beer
is served. This shows a change in the principles for mobilizing communal
labour. With the removal of beer, the gatherings of this *hakuma* are of
shorter duration than the ordinary parties, and the extensive ritual is itself changing. Instead of ending because the beer is finished, the migrants' *hakuma* ends with the members praying together and then leaving. Furthermore, respect for the grade system is not very strong in this
hakuma. One will find roughly the same people sitting together, but no
police guarding the *mudiria* and *zeriba al malik*, and people will move
around freely between the groups. Old people do not take the rituals of
this *hakuma* seriously either. Thus the migrants may call to older men

Table 9.   *Grades used in the hakuma*

zeriba al malik

malik (Arab.),	king.
sir al dar (sirdar) (Arab.),	used for commander in chief of Egyptian army
hakim al am (Arab.)	Governor General
sekreter qadaya (Arab.),	secretary in a court case
shawish "englisi" (Arab.),	an English sergeant
doktor,	medical doctor
sekreter amelia (Arab.),	secretary of a medical operation

mudiria

mudir (Arab.),	manager
neib al mudir,	assistant manager
jenabo (Arab.),	term used for person with authority
sol (Turk.), (*Sol qol aghasi*),	lit. commander of the left wing—used in the Sudan Defence Force and Sudanese police of warrant officer
jenabo al mufattish (Arab.),	*mufattish* is an inspector
sarraf (Arab.),	cashier
dabit al majlis (Arab.),	administrative officer in a council
dabit al polis (Arab.),	police officer
mamur (Arab.),	lit. ordered. Used in the Sudan of a Governor of a province from the beginning of Egyptian rule til 1933. Later a civilian administration assistant to a District Commissioner
askeri (Arab.),	soldier
morassla (Arab.),	messenger

khabat

mudir al khabat (Arab.),	manager of forestry department
luwa (Arab.),	general
kommandant,	commander
dabit (Arab.),	officer
mufattish khabat (Arab.),	forestry inspector
dabit al berak (Arab.),	officer of the flag
al bey (Turk.),	civil and military title immediately below that of Pasha
askeri	(see above)
morassla	(see above)

dobbat

sekreter amelia	(see above)
sarraf	(see above)

See also Hill, R. 1967, *A Biographical Dictionary of the Sudan* walking by and invite them in for a meal; but they seldom pay attention to this. In a "proper" *hakuma*, such a failure to react to an invitation would result in the person being brought in by the "police" and charged with showing contempt for the *hakuma*. Thus not only is the principle of mobilization changing, but also the very nature of the *hakuma* rituals is changing and declining in importance.

CHANGES IN THE LAFOFA USE OF BEER

While doing field-work among the Lafofa, I also observed some processes that may show us how the connotation of symbols changes as a result of the ways people adapt, thus enabling us to establish some causal relationships in the process of change. The changes I refer to relate to the use of beer (*marissa*) among the Lafofa.

The role of beer in this society is of great importance, it is used to mobilize labour for cultivation, housebuilding and other activities that require communal effort. Beer is also important to those who make it, the women. When a woman makes her first beer, this is a subject of conversation among the men, and they will go to taste it. Once I participated on such an occasion in which the men cracked jokes to the husband of the beer-maker, saying the beer did not taste like beer should and that they would be better off drinking beer somewhere else. In the end, however, the beer was praised and the husband was told he had a good wife. Once established as a beer-maker a woman will sell beer and make an income from it in addition to earning an income from mat-braiding and perhaps from her own cultivation.

Beer is not just significant in such immediate and economic contexts. Beer was an integral part of all the ritual occasions described in Chapters 2 and 3. The fact that these have disappeared and have been replaced by Islamic ones means that beer should have no place in them. However, one incident during the Islamic festival *Id al Dahia* demonstrates the role of beer.

During this festival, the Islamic believers among the Lafofa visited each other to eat meat in each other's houses, as is common among other Sudanese. They went to pray on the first morning of the *Id*, with the Qadiriyya *sheikh*, then returned home to visit each other. The old men in the village, however, did not join in these activities. They stayed at home during the first two days of the festival. But then, on the third and fourth days, these old-timers started visiting each other's houses, sharing beer instead of meat.

Another indication of how important beer is in bringing people together I observed in relation to selling and paying for meat. When cattle fall down from rocks on the mountain and break their legs, they must be slaughtered immediately. In such cases people come to buy meat from the owner, but they rarely have the money to pay cash. Later on the collection of money becomes a problem for the owner of the animal since people will try to postpone further payment. Collecting money on an individual basis is next to impossible, because fifty to sixty people are involved. In such a case the seller of the meat will choose a day on which to gather all the people. He tells them that he has made beer and that they should come and pay him.

Apart from mobilizing people for labour, then, beer serves as a mobilizing medium in several other contexts as well. The beer that people drink at social gatherings is different from the beer that is sold. When women make beer for sale, they will filter it to remove all the grain. The buyers get clear beer and drink it as it is. The beer for work parties as well as other social occasions is not filtered but all the grain is left in it. While drinking, people refill their beer pots with water, thus making it last longer.

The above presentation shows that beer is important among the Lafofa and serves as an idiom on several levels of Lafofa society. When the migrants stop using it and their wives stop making it this has important repercussions.

It is my argument that the migrants' behaviour and their choice of idioms to express their identities must be seen as a result of the ways they adapt to a wider arena in Liri, not only to the local Lafofa scene. On the wider scene, the Lafofa face certain handicaps. Nuba is in itself a derogatory term and there is a stigma on the Nuba identity. In Liri, the stereotype of a Nuba living in a mountain village or elsewhere portrays him as a beer-drinking, non-Muslim. Any Lafofa who wants to be accepted into a wider Sudanese society will have to deal with this stereotype. One way of doing it is through signalling non-drinking, seclusion of women and a public display of Islamic identities.

It is true that Islam puts negative sanctions on drinking alcohol and that the drinking of *marissa* is frowned upon, but it is also a fact that many Arabic groups also use it to mobilize labour and on other occasions. But in such areas the Arab farmers have been Islamized since the early days of Islam in the Sudan and do not have to deal with any stigma on their identity. The significance of drinking beer is different in such groups.

The Lafofa live in a frontier area in which Islamization and the opening up of society is an ongoing, contemporary process. The signalling of an Islamic and Sudanese identity is, therefore, crucial in the latter case. One effective way to signal this change is to renounce a prime idiom of traditional Lafofa identity, which at the same time is part of their stigmatized identity, that of beer-drinking.

Before we continue, let us halt and explore some of the consequences of the removal of beer. One way of doing this is to look more closely at some situations in which beer has been important and to compare them with the new situation without beer.

Let us start with a description of a normal drinking session, in which people come to a house to buy *marissa*. The beer is brought in small pots, *abar*, and then poured into bigger pots. The number of people drinking from such a pot may vary, but there is a clear pattern of friends and relatives drinking together. What happens is that a man, on his arrival, will buy a small *abar*, pour it into the larger one and join in the drinking. A newcomer who does not "belong" may be denied permission to join in the pot and may start drinking alone. Drinking is an expression of relationships, with people sitting in circles with friends and relatives.

If we turn to a communal work group, the same pattern will be seen, though there are a variety of work groups among the Lafofa, this pattern may also be more elaborate. One example is the *hakuma* work group with its big, formalized group of some 30 people, with fixed labour input and a highly ritualized organization that shapes the way people work as well as the way they organize themselves for common beer-drinking after the work is done. The grade system in such a *hakuma* makes people not only sit in small circles but sit together with people of the same grade. This layout is shown in Figure 9 and, apart from the general organization, one should note that those who are not members of a *hakuma* but still come to drink will be termed Arabs and placed some distance away from the others.

Compare this with the lay-out of a *karama*, which in many ways is the counterpart of a beer session, within an Islamic context. An animal is slaughtered and while the food is being prepared, people sit around, waiting and chatting. The old-timers who attend the beer sessions will not be there this time. Migrants will make up the audience and a *faqi* will be invited. When the food is ready, people will gather to eat it and then drink tea. There is no system determining who eats together, nor are there rules about who sits where. The *karama* can be said to express equality and unity, not among the Lafofa compared to the Arabs, but for the Lafofa as part of a wider context of Muslims.

This religious context is expressed through the ritual slaughtering of an animal. It is also expressed through the praying and the ending of a *karama* with a *fateh*. The *faqi* is the leader of all these activities and if other people are there, they will not be placed "outside" as "marginal" Arabs, but will take part on an equal basis. If Arabs are present, they will be important participants in such rituals, because they know the prayers and the religious content better than the Lafofa. I have observed a *karama* where no *faqi* attended, the reciting of the *fateh* at the end breaking down in laughter, because nobody knew the words. Instead of the Arabs being classified as outsiders, as happens in the *hakuma*, Arabs in the *karama* become central agents of a code the Lafofa do not fully command, thus underlining the inferiority of the Lafofa in the wider realm of the Muslim world.

This pattern becomes significant because the migrants and their women consciously refuse to take part in the occasions organized around beer drinking. They also seek out *karama* situations, both to meet fellow migrants and to talk to the *faqi*, but also as a conscious signalling of a new identity. With the systematic exposure to events that contain communicative messages like those elaborated above, one might expect the connotations of symbols to change and thereby their users' general outlook on life. This is a result of different groups of Lafofa embracing new values and idioms, thereby seeking other arenas to express their identities and becoming exposed to the different dynamics of those various arenas. I have indicated earlier that this is an effect of some Lafofa pursuing new economic strategies that lead them into closer contact with the regional population of Liri than is the case with older Lafofa, who pursue more traditional strategies.

7. Maintenance and change of Lafofa cultural traditions

The discussion in Chapter 6 shows one way of establishing the dynamic relationships that link codification processes to interactional systems. Using the same conceptual scheme, we may now address other changes that have occurred in the Lafofa way of life, which must also be seen as effects of the ways individual Lafofa adapted to a wider socio-cultural environment. My intention, then, is to return to the discussion in Chapters 2 and 3 and try to elucidate some of the dynamics that may explain the changes we outlined there. It is also necessary, at this point, to relate the discussion more explicitly to theoretical concepts and to the analytical outline presented in the General Introduction. The first part, however, is based on the empirical material presented earlier.

MATRILINY AND CHANGE

One conclusion drawn from my discussion in Chapter 3, on how the matrilineal system of the Lafofa has changed, is that we cannot discuss the total matrilineal system as it enters a total modern system. The discussion showed that the matrilineal system should not be seen as a single entity, which changes all at once.

This point is also borne out in other studies. In a study from West Sumatra, Kato (1981) has shown how principles of matrilineality among the Minangkabau have been adapted to times and circumstances also characterized by increasing economic development. The changes in one aspect of the system (e.g. inheritance) have not been followed by changes in others (e.g. descent). And inheritance has changed for personal property but not for ancestral property. Thus Kato asks whether there is a change at all in the matrilineal system as such, or whether inheritance practices have become more elaborate, without foregoing the matrilineal principle. Again, the point is not to make use of logically integrated systems that have to change as total systems, but rather of specific elements that derive their meaning from their specific position in such systems. This is dependent on how people act and "make use of" their social organization. With such a perspective, we can discuss how the matrilineal "constraints" are *selectively* losing their hold on people. We may ask "what people?" and "why?", thereby tying our description to what people do in other fields of their lives.

FROM DESCENT TO KINSHIP

The fading corporate status of the Lafofa matriline in the context of modernization is also a development borne out by earlier studies. Kathleen Gough has the following to say about which effects the modernization process has had on matrilineal societies

> Recent literature has accumulated evidence to show that under economic changes brought about by contact with Western industrial nations, matrilineal descent groups gradually disintegrate. In their place, the elementary family eventually emerges as the key kinship group with respect to residence, economic cooperation, legal responsibility and socialization, with a narrow range of interpersonal kinship relationships spreading outward from it bilaterally and linking it with other elementary families. (Gough, 1961:631)

Evidence for this trend is found among various African groups like the Tonga (Colson, 1958), the Ndembu (Turner, 1957), the Yao (Mitchell, 1956), the Bemba (Richards, 1939, 1950) and the Ashanti (Fortes, 1949). They all seem to argue that increasing wealth and economic differentiation weaken the principle of matrilineal descent, by excluding matrilineal cousins from inheritance and passing it on to sons instead of sister's sons. Similarly they all seem to regard the elementary family as the basic group of society.

My point is that what is happening among the Lafofa is a development away from descent, i.e. an ancestor oriented principle of organization, to a kinship system classified among "egocentric systems of social identities and statuses" (Scheffler, 1966: 756). I want to argue that the processes of integration will further fuel a development towards nuclear families, as joint households and assets are transferred from fathers to sons. Women will be more confined to their houses and become more "domestic"; those having maternal relatives to support them will have a greater ability to resist this than women with only brothers, who are also migrants, as their closest family. Over time, however, the process will lead to the Lafofa domestic unit becoming more similar to that of their Sudanese neighbours.

Given the problems the Lafofa kinship system and kin term system caused the migrants, who wanted to relate to the regional scene, as we saw in Chapter 6, we may also speculate whether the reproduction of the Lafofa kin system will deteriorate and whether new conceptualizations based on the Arabic way of thinking will gain a stronger position.

TRANSITION CEREMONIES AS IDENTITY MARKERS

Some of the basic changes among the Lafofa in the wake of their integration into the Sudanese state relate to concepts of physical and sexual shame and to their transition ceremonies. Marriage changed from a small ceremonial event, with young people arranging their own love affairs. If two people decided to marry, they would tell their parents who would normally accept it. A girl would go on living with her mother until after her first child was born. During this period the husband would work for his wife's people in bride-service. After the first child was born, a house would be built for the couple on the land of the husband's people. The beer for this work would be provided by the wife's side, although many others would take part in the actual building. In case of divorce, which was frequent, the man would keep the house, while his wife would move to the house of a new husband, taking the children with her (Seligman, 1932).

The introduction of bride-price instead of bride-service and the elaborate ceremonial occasions around the marriage are new developments. Marriage customs common in Central Sudan have been adopted since the 1940s and give marriage an economic dimension it did not have before, forcing young men to earn money for this purpose. Building the couple's first house has become the responsibility of the young man, not the bride's family as before. Divorce has also become more problematic since a man will not get back his money if he himself initiates a divorce. A woman who wants to get a divorce has to pay back twice the sum of the bride-price which, with the sums involved today, is virtually impossible without help from relatives.

Age-group organization also used to be important among the Lafofa. Shortly after puberty the boys would spend the rainy season taking care of cattle and would live in cattle kraals. At the end of such a period of seclusion a dance would be performed by those involved. To take part in this dance a boy had to have undergone three periods of seclusion during three rainy seasons. The mothers' brothers of the boys would play an active role in the ceremonies that followed the dancing. The young men who went through this ceremony together stood in a special relationship to each other. They would hunt together, help each other in daily work and, if no incest rules prevented it, would marry each other's sisters. These young men would also dominate the ceremonial wrestling matches that were held after harvest time.

For the girls there were also such markers to signal the change from childhood to womanhood. Unlike in many other Nuba societies (Nadel, 1947) there does not seem to have existed any seclusion ceremonies for Lafofa girls after their first menstruation. But Seligman indicates that ceremonial wrestling matches for girls may have corresponded to the ceremonial beating of the boys. At that particular time the girls also had their bodies scarred. After a girl had her first child, she would not wrestle again, but during that first pregnancy more of her face and body would be covered with scars.

The age-grade system has also declined and is no longer a living institution. The seclusion periods no longer exist, and the transition ceremony that might correspond to the ones described above would be the one of circumcision. Both boys and girls are now circumcised.

Some notes on the dynamics of change

Today any Lafofa would agree that marrying in a "modern" way and performing circumcision are basic elements of any person's identity and all Lafofa comply with them, no matter how Arabized or Islamized they are. It is interesting, however, to note that these changes started as individual strategies. People who had contact with the government in the 1920's would start putting on clothes and gradually adopted practices such as circumcision. This was partly a strategy to gain prestige through adopting the ways of the dominant groups of society in Central Sudan. Similarly, it was only in the 1940s that the marriage customs started to be introduced.

In my opinion, their turning into universally valid and accepted customs is related to the need of a group like the Lafofa, living among Islamic and Arabic groups, to signal a basic human quality. An important premise for the slave hunting period, in which the Nuba were a target for slave hunting expeditions, was the categorization of the slave population as not being human. Legally they were classified together with cattle and other animals (Spaulding, 1982:12). With increasing contact, which for the Lafofa started in the late 1920s, they needed to deal with this. As the above customs are basic to concepts of human decency among their neighbours, they become useful markers to express human qualities. They are general requirements, not a matter of individual belief or choice.

THE NEW MEANING OF WRESTLING

A second example, relating to the development of ceremonial wrestling among the Lafofa, can further help underline my point. Wrestling was related to the harvest season and for girls it also represented a transition ceremony. Today wrestling exists in Liri, but for boys only. No girl ever wrestles. We have seen that wrestling for boys has changed from being organized according to membership in the matrilineal descent groups and is today organized regionally, with a number of villages making up one team. Wrestling has also become a sport for the Arabs in Liri. Wrestling is thus an example of an old sport still practiced, but with a new cultural content and new participants. I have argued that its continuation may be related to the fact that wrestling celebrates important values of strength and manhood that are shared by the Lafofa and the Arabs.

If we compare this with the development of female wrestling, we see that the latter has disappeared altogether. This disappearance I ascribed to the need of the Lafofa to relate to society at large and to express basic human qualities in the way they were being expressed in the surrounding world. Female wrestling stands in much stronger opposition to these notions about womanhood than does male wrestling to Arabic notions of manhood.

Female wrestling thus assumes a similar position to nakedness and traditional transition ceremonies in that its discontinuation is not a matter of individual choice, but of basic human decency. Once they are accepted, however, we may apply Victor Turner's point about *rites de passage* not being individual rituals only, but rituals that concern total societies. Especially the liminal phases represent, according to Turner, "a realm of pure possibility whence novel configurations of ideas and relations may arise" (Turner, 1967:96–97). Although Turner's main concern is with the symbolic possibilities of all this, I think such rites of passage would offer structurally ideal situations for the introduction of other types of Islamic connotations. Such rites, once they have been accepted, thus become vehicles of further Islamization.

THE SIGNIFICANCE OF NEW RITUAL FORMS

The above point is further underlined because such rites bring new ritual leaders onto the scene, replacing old ones, and such ritual occasions thereby help to reproduce certain relationships, while others lose their significance. This is particularly evident in the way the traditional ritual expert, the *kujor*, has declined in importance and has been replaced by the Islamic holy man, the *faqi*.

These developments are of far-reaching importance for the ways Lafofa cultural traditions are reproduced and changed. The old rituals were all occasions on which several levels of Lafofa social and ritual life coalesced and could be expressed and reinforced. Furthermore, the ritual cycle was organized around the cultivation cycle, tying together economic and ritual life. The *kujor* was the pivotal point around whom all this revolved, and his house was an important spatial centre for this ritual life.

Compare this to the organization and lay-out of the Islamic rituals that are dominant among the Lafofa today. They are organized around the five daily prayers and the important Friday prayer, the month of fasting, Ramadan, and the pilgrimage to Mecca. The local Islam of Liri revolves around the Qadiriyya centre and the leading *sheikh* there and from this brotherhood come the *faqi* that have replaced the *kujor*.

The Qadiriyya in Liri thus appears as a ritual and organizational unit with the great *sheikh* at the pivotal point, and with lesser *sheikhs* as his representatives. This network of dervishes is very important for teaching illiterate people about Islam. The teaching of Muhamed and the content of the Koran are transferred by direct contact between a *sheikh* and his followers. To a Lafofa being a Muslim thus means going to the places where the teaching goes on, be they at a *noba* dance, a *karama*, a wedding in the village, or a *mesid*.

The teaching in such encounters contains various elements of direct relevance for the daily life of the Lafofa. A central theme is what is lawful (*halal*) and what is forbidden (*haram*) in Islam. People are told that beer-making and beer-drinking is *haram* and not tolerated. They are told that women should be protected and not allowed to go shopping or selling produce and that young daughters should be married before their virginity is endangered. In general terms the Lafofa gain knowledge about Islamic standards and can use this knowledge to evaluate themselves and others in relationship to the central issue of whether or not to be a Muslim.

In this respect the migrants have a special position among the Lafofa. They are among the most active in attending occasions where there is Islamic teaching. When they return from Khartoum, they each hold a *karama* to celebrate their safe homecoming and invite the Lafofa *faqi* to attend. They also invite the *faqi* privately, to come and spend the day drinking tea and coffee and eating with them.

Old people do not take part in this unless they are closely related to the individuals involved. An elderly person's daily life is thus largely without contact with these types of activities. They come to eat the *karama*, but having drunk beer, they do not pray and usually leave before the final prayer, *al fateh*.

An important conclusion is therefore that the changes we have described lead to changes in important encounters in which basic socio-cultural relationships and their content are expressed. Changes in such encounters also imply changes in the messages that are communicated and thus form a basis for the development of new concepts about the world.

THEORETICAL CONSIDERATIONS

We now have to return to the theoretical approach that I outlined in the introduction to this book. In that discussion I underlined some points of importance for the perspective I have used to understand my Lafofa material. In the following I want to raise these points again as I think we now have a better basis for showing further implications that follow from those points.

Symbols in historical contexts

Throughout this book I have pointed out that we should not look at a total Lafofa social and cultural system as against a total Sudanese one. This also holds for how we perceive the matrilineal system. Our description of changes has shown that we do not observe a single homogeneous process of change, but rather a complex process in which some "traditional" elements remain, while new ones appear. Furthermore, we cannot establish a new unity in which contemporary Lafofa society and culture is depicted as an integrated whole. Nor can we speculate about cultural continuity, assuming that the symbols we see today are transformations of earlier ones (e.g. that today's avoidance of pork, and beer "is" the same as earlier food taboos).

To address this problem I argued that we should look at society as a collection of practices, symbols, and codes that are used in situations of interaction. People take up new practices and abandon others not so much as a planned process, but rather as a result of their wider life situation. My aim has been not to depict an integrated system that might be called Lafofa culture, but to build up an explanation of how *some* elements can be seen to develop *within the context of other elements*.

We have seen throughout this book that to an increasing degree the total life situation of the Lafofa is formed by their participation in wider economic and social arenas in which the cultural competence and the ways the Lafofa organize their lives are not very relevant in defining what occurs in those arenas. There is a need for the Lafofa to deal with such situations, particularly as the Nuba have a stigmatized identity in the wider Sudanese society. Such arenas and society at large provide opportunities for the Lafofa. Involvement in new economic careers and utilization of new investment opportunities have in Chapter 5 been shown to put migrants in a better economic situation locally than that of those who are more depedant on local resources. The local Liri situation, with the *jellaba* traders leaving the consumer trade for mechanized farming, has opened up investment possibilities beyond the "normal" petty trade level. The need for an acceptable identity is thus also present.

The dynamics of the acceptance and rejection of symbols among the Lafofa must be seen in this context. But such arenas are also dynamic, and the content and the "climate" of interaction is not static. The early history of integration, during the first half of this century, provided a different context for interaction than does the contemporary one, in which the process of Sudanization is dominant and in which the "demands" for a particular code of conduct are stronger. We have shown how this has led to changes developing differently among the Lafofa. To oversimplify, we may say that what the Lafofa were communicating to the environment during the first period of integration, during which transition

ceremonies changed, was that "we are human beings". The later developments, including the rejection of beer and pressure on the domestication
of women, are more like saying, "we are credit-worthy, we can play the
same game as you". What type of idioms will change as a result of such
processes will be influenced by how useful the symbols are for expressing
that particular message. They are not "continuations" of old forms, but
new dynamic inventions formed by such criteria of usefulness.

The significance of encounters of interaction

We cannot reduce the changes we have seen nor the processes behind
them to a level at which individuals pursue their own strategies and adapt
in particular ways in the process, although I do maintain that these are
important starting points for our explanation. Reproduction of culture is
also a collective process and we are faced with the problem of explaining
how the new symbols become shared, that is, how some become socially
significant, whereas others die out. To do this we need to expatiate on
how *encounters of interaction* may work to convey meaning, that is, to look
into "the communicative effects of events" (Barth, 1987:78).

I have tried to describe in detail some of the events that I observed and
believe I can relate to the changes I saw. Particularly my analysis of local
cultivation, of communal work groups and of the declining importance
of beer was meant to contribute to this. The differences I pointed out between the old ritual occasions and the modern Islamic ones serve the
same purpose. My point in doing this was to show that such events can be
seen as "texts" with inherent meaning from which participants draw their
understanding, but that the participants themselves also *confer* meaning
on such events, depending on who they are. This is important, because
such events and encounters are more than individual occasions shaped
by immediate needs and contexts. Some are "charged with meaning" in
the sense that the structure and organization of the encounters provide
us with important leads as to how the underlying social and cultural structures are constituted. Such structures "are" in the events themselves. To
further clarify this let me return to the description of the Lafofa as presented in Chapter 2.

In the early parts of this century the Lafofa were living in a context of
corporate matrilineal clans with strong age-organizations. Ritual experts
organized a ritual life that consisted of secret rain rituals in which knowledge obtained by the *kujor* was inherited from the ancestors. This revolved around the agricultural cycle, thus combining economic activities
and social organization with ritual life and a basic Lafofa cosmology. We
do not have detailed information about it, but I believe that participation
in this type of life must have influenced the Lafofa as a people and as individuals. I do not mean that everybody had the same understanding of

what was going on. Mothers' brothers would see things differently from sisters' sons, men from women, old people from young people, ritual leaders from ordinary people, and so on. Hence different groups would confer different meanings on the events of which we are speaking. Yet I think that there would be sufficient common understanding among the people to generate a Lafofa way of life, as I have tried to depict it in Chapter 2.

If we now move to contemporary Lafofa society, we can keep the same perspective on things, but the empirical picture that emerges is different. We have said many times that the integration process has brought new realities to the Lafofa and we have described and analysed some important processes that could show this, including work parties, beer-drinking, and so on. We have also seen that events are meaningful to participants, but even more significant has been the dramatic *difference* in the ways different people have acted and perceived the content of rituals. It is in this difference in understanding, and meaning conferred on the situations, that I seek an important dynamic of change.

Migrants stood out as one significant group who conferred a different meaning on such occasions than did the old-timers. From that difference in meaning new elements emerged, and changed the organization of communal work groups among the Lafofa in significant ways. Similarly, we see how the attitude to beer and its place on various occasions differs, with the old men bringing it to the Islamic festival "*Id al Dahia*" on the third day, thus "accepting" that it did not belong to the religious context, but "smuggling" it in at a later stage of the celebrations.

The dynamic of this is related to the discussion in the section above, in which the migrants are that group of Lafofa which can benefit from new opportunities and for which the identity game vis-à-vis the surrounding world is most significant in determining their success or failure in those new strategies. The pursuit of similar strategies, which leads to involvement in similar types of arenas and encounters, helps to develop similarities in their outlook on the world and thus confers similar types of meaning on what goes on in their home area. "Agreeing" that beer is bad, on the need to control women, on the fact that old ideas are superstitions only, all help to influence how people form their interaction among themselves, vis-à-vis other Lafofa and vis-à-vis non-Lafofa. People's understanding is thus carried over from one situation to the other.

The future of the Lafofa cultural traditions

The perspective outlined above has implications for the prospects of the Lafofa to preserve a distinct cultural tradition. It is certain that the processes described in this book are reducing the cultural distinctiveness of the Lafofa tradition. This process will continue, I believe, because an im-

portant part of the dynamic behind these changes is that of individua
Lafofa dealing with their marginality and their stigmatized identity in
wider Sudanese context. What I see is a continuous emptying of tradi
tional Lafofa symbols of their meanings, traditional values, beliefs an
expressions and, in the process, becoming classified as "superstition" an
"backwardness". At this level I see the Lafofa tradition disappearing, be
cause the basic elements within which Lafofa culture was reproduced ar
also changing. I refer here to the changes in matrilineality and its expres
sions.

The socio-cultural changes discussed among the Lafofa also affect th
basic process of being a social person in that group. The young Lafof
grow up differently from the old Lafofa. What the young migrants fin
personally compelling is very different from what is compelling for th
old-timers. Concepts about the world, about themselves and about thei
place in the world are all elements that must look very different to
young Lafofa than to the elderly Lafofa. This relates to the basic differ
ences in the central concepts of the Lafofa cultural tradition compared t
a Sudanese, Arabic or Islamic one. The two systems are differently or
ganized both as social organizations and in the way cultural content i
structured. The differences I focus on are similar to the ones referred t
by Jack Goody when he discusses literacy in society (Goody, 1968, 1986
and also by Fredrik Barth when he relates such differences to the con
cepts of Great Traditions and Little Traditions (Barth, 1982, 1983
1987).

Some of the dynamics in the process of change can be seen to be influ
enced by differences beween oral traditions, as exemplified by th
Lafofa, and a literary tradition exemplified by the Arabic, Islamic an
Sudanese. The knowledge produced in the old Lafofa system was oral
expressed in communal rituals, sanctioned by relations to ancestors an
intertwined with the process of building social persons who belonged t
matrilines, exogamous groups of *imbie*, age-grades and so on. In the sam
manner as Barth argues about the Baktaman, I think we may say that t
a large extent this knowledge lies in the *whole society*.

In the modern context knowledge is different, and the reproduction o
knowledge is different. The Islamic *faqis* represent *teachers* of the hol
scripture, they are *missionaries* who are spreading a religious message con
tained in the Koran. The situations in which this occurs are structured b
the written message in quite a different way from the earlier ritual occa
sions. Knowledge is in the book, and specialists transfer the knowledg
through teaching. This difference in means of communication betwee
the two traditions is significant. The quarrel that developed at the wed
ding in Chapter 3 may serve as a small example to illustrate this. Th
reaction to the young migrants who brought a written list of what shoul
be presented to the bride's family was very negative. I interpret this as sig

nifying people's reaction towards attempts to fix something that was flexble in the old days. The difficulties experienced by the young Lafofa in he *mahkama* court when explaining their relationships to other people to in Arabic and Muslim audience point in the same direction.

There are basic differences in the ways the two systems are constituted and in the knowledge that is obtained from either. People living within hese systems will develop different notions about the world and about vho they are. By consciously seeking occasions and events in which they ict and behave "as Arabs" they expose themselves and accept "the vast, elf-confirming structure of law, politics and property, supported by a pattern of domestic organization and daily activity" (Barth, 1987:56–57) hat characterizes Middle East societies.

This does not mean that I am describing a conflict-ridden society in crisis and internal contradiction. Although we can talk about various "sub-traditions" and isolate them in the way we have done for the migrants, people still interact and cooperate, whether they are migrants or pld-timers. They share a common understanding of the world in a way hat makes interaction easy. The old people "understand" the new ways, as the migrants do some old customs, so that they can interact intelligibly. The difference is in the extent to which they embrace those ideas and hus to what degree they make various types of concepts relevant in their pwn lives.

Furthermore, the changes we are talking about do not affect the Lafofa as a social category in Liri. All who are born Lafofa still consider themselves members of that group. This ethnic identity is reproduced hrough the Lafofa still primarily marrying within their own group and hrough patterns of residence. The Lafofa either live in the mountain villages or in special Lafofa quarters in the plains villages, like other groups lo. The political framework[1], with the Lafofa being defined as a group with its own political leadership, also helps to reproduce Lafofa identity. As we saw from the *mahkama*, to some extent the legal system respects Lafofa notions of ownership and allows old, knowledgeable men to decide in such matters.

---

1. The contemporary situation in the Sudan as depicted in the Preface may of course change this, and create new political opportunities for the Lafofa as well as other Nuba people to reorganize their communities and also open for new avenues of participation in public arenas in the Sudan.

Glossary

Anthropological terms

age-grade	a social category based on age, within a series of such categories through which individuals pass in the course of their life cycles
bilateral descent	descent traced through both father and mother
bride-price	marriage payments from the husband and his kin to the bride's kin
bride-service	a husband's work and services for the bride's kin
clan	a unilineal descent group or category whose members trace descent from an apical ancestor/ancestress, but do not know the genealogical links that connect them to this ancestor
classificatory kinship	a mode of kinship classification in which the relatives in earlier generations are terminologically equal (father's brother = father, mother's sister = mother)
descent	a relationship defined by connection to an ancestor (or ancestress) through a culturally recognized sequence of parent–child links (from father to son to son's son = patrilineal descent; from mother to daughter to daughter's daughter = matrilineal descent)
ego	person taken to be focal point for the reckoning of relationships in systems of kinship terminology
exogamy	a requirement that marriage takes place outside a particular social group or range of kinship
genealogy	a pedigree; a web of relationships traced through parents and children
incest taboo	a rule prohibiting sexual relations between immediate kin and others culturally in equivalent relationships (differs from exogamy which prohibits marriage but not necessarily sexual relations)
matrilineal	a principle of descent from an ancestress through her daughter, her daughter's daughter and so on (in the female line)
patrilineal	descent traced through a line of ancestors in the male line
rite de passage	a ritual dramatizing the transition from one social status to another
segmentary	of descent systems, defining descent categories with reference to more and more remote apical ancestors
unilineal	descent through one line, i.e. patrilineal or matrilineal descent

Arabic terms

abar	small pot; vessel for measuring *marissa*
abid	slave
abu	father
akho	brother
alim	learned person possessing religious knowledge
am	father's brother
ama	father's sister
asida	porridge made of sorghum
baraka	blessing, divine power possessed by certain people
baramka	organization among Baggara men; especially for tea-drinking
belila	roasted or boiled grain
bey (Turkish)	equivalent to *sayyid*, i.e. honorable man
bint	girl, daughter of
birish	raided mat
bi'sm'Allahi	"in the name of God"
botton	womb
dabit (pl. *dobbat*)	officer
dar	home territory of tribal group
dhikr	religious dance
angrib	bed
faqi (pl. *fuqara*)	Islamic "Holy Man", particularly religious person
fateh	Islamic blessing
feddan	square measure, 1.04 acres, 0.42 hectare
fellata	Sudanese term for West African people
ghazwa	organization for slave raiding
gabil	square measure, 500 square meters
haboba	grandmother
hafir	basin for collecting rainwater, dam
haj	person having undertaken the pilgrimage to Mecca
hakuma	government, term used for labour organization
halal	what is legal within Islam
haram	what is forbidden within Islam
haqq	right
hariq	fire
hurr	free, a free man as opposed to slave
id	religious festival
id al dahia	the big *bayram*. Sacrificial celebration in Islam
id al fitr/Ramadan	celebration marking the end of *Ramadan*, the month of fasting
jebel	mountain
jellaba	trader
jidd	grandfather
jihadiyya	slave army
jubraka	cultivated plots on the mountainsides
karama	feast expressing gratitude to Allah
khabat	forestry department
khal	mother's brother

khala	mother's sister
khalifa	"successor", ruler of the Muslim community
khalwa	religious school, Koranic school
khasm bait	minimal lineage
kubbaniyya	organization for slave raiding
kuttab	school
koshuq	shops made of zinc
lejna	committee
lubia	beans
mahdi	"the guided one"—reference to the Sudanese *mahdi* who ruled the country from 1880–85
mahkama	local court
malik	king
maliki	civilized
marissa	sorghum beer
mek	tribal leader among the Nuba, equivalent of *omda*
mesid	religious center
midd	measure of capacity, 5 litres
mudir	director, governor
mudiria	province
mufattish	inspector
mullah	sauce used on *asida*
muwallid	born in the Sudan
nafir	work organization, group work
nazir	tribal leader, above *omda* and *mek*
nebbi	prophet
noba	religious drum
omda	tribal leader, equivalent of *mek*
qadi	judge
rakuba	a roof on poles for shade
ras	head
rotl	measure of weight, 12 *waqia* = 449.28 g.
safiha	tin bucket
schela	things provided by groom before marriage
shail	a credit relationship
sharia	Islamic law
sheikh	tribal or village leader, below *omda* and *mek*
sherif	religious man, based on learning
sufi	religious man, part of Islamic brotherhood
suq	marketplace
takarir	generic term for person of West African origin
tariqa	Islamic brotherhood
taube	headcloth used by women
turak (Turkish)	unit in Turkish army
teht	under
ukht	sister
ulema	(Board of-) men of high religious learning within Islam (jurists
um	mother

mma	the Muslim "nation"
ad	boy, son of
akil	assistant, deputy
ahid	one
aqia	measure of weight, 1.32 ounces = 37.44 g.
riba	corral made of thorn bushes
rqa	used about black, non-Arab groups in North Sudan

afofa terms

ame	term for a young man who has had his first child
amelai	a ritual dance
amenai	age-set, those who can marry
ujor	rain-maker
were	cattle kraal
nambie	mother's sister
nani	mother
nba	father
nbabie	father's brother, father's sister
nbie	brother, sister
nbige	grandparents
nbing	mother's brother, sister's son
mbing	age-set, old men

udanese currency

| t. | Piastre |
| S | Sudanese pounds, £S1 = 100 Pt. |

Bibliography

Abakr, Abdel Rahman, 1977. *Development and Administration in Southern Darfur* Unpublished Ph.D. Thesis, Sussex University: IDS.

Abrahams, R.G., 1965. "Neighbourhood Organizations: A Major System Among the Northern Nyamwezi", *Africa*, 35

Ahmed, Abbas, 1980. *White Nile Arabs. Political Leadership and Economic Change* London: Athlone.

Ahmed, Abdel Ghaffar M., 1974. *Shaykhs and Followers. Political Struggle in the Rufa'a al-Hoi Nazirate in the Sudan*. Khartoum: Khartoum University Press.

Ahmed, Abdel Ghaffar M. (ed.), 1976, *Some Aspects of Pastoral Nomadism in the Sudan*. Khartoum: Khartoum University Press.

Ahmed, Abdel Ghaffar M. with Mustafa A. Rahman, 1979. "Small Urban Centers: Vanguards of Exploitation: Two Cases from Sudan". *Africa*, 49 (3).

Al Assam, Mukhtar n.d., *Decentralization in the Sudan*. Khartoum: Ministry of Culture and Information.

Allan, W., 1965. *The African Husbandman*. Westport, Greenwood Press.

Alpers, E.A., 1972. "Towards a History of the Expansion of Islam in East Africa the Matrilineal People of the Southern Interior", in T.O. Ranger and I.N Kimambo (eds.), *The Historical Study of African Religion*. London: UMI.

Arber, H.B., 1940. "The Baramka". *SNR*, XXIII.

Asad, T., 1970. *The Kababish Arabs. Power, Authority and Consent in a Nomadic Tribe* London: C. Hurst.

Asad, T., 1986. *The Idea of An Anthropology of Islam*. Georgetown University Center for Contemporary Arab Studies.

Awadalla, S.A., 1985. *Tegale District, Southern Kordofan* (Sudan). Monitoring Report, no. 2. Khartoum: Institute for Environmental Studies.

Barbour, K.M., 1961. *The Republic of the Sudan. A Regional Geography*. London London University Press.

Barlett, P., 1980. "Adaptive Strategies in Peasant Agricultural Production", *Annual Review of Anthropology*, Vol. 9.

Barth, F., 1964. "Competition and Symbiosis in North-East Baluchistan", *Folk*, 6.

Barth, F., 1966. *Models of Social Organization*. London: The Royal Anthropological Institute.

Barth, F., 1967 a). *Human Resources*. Bergen: Bergen Studies in Social Anthropology, No.1.

Barth, F. 1967 b). "Economic Spheres in Darfur", in R. Firth (ed.), *Themes in Economic Anthropology*. London: Tavistock.

Barth, F. (ed.), 1969. *Ethnic Groups and Boundaries. The Social Organization of Culture Difference*. Bergen: Norwegian University Press.

Barth, F., 1970. *Sociological Aspects of Integrated Surveys for River Basin Development*. Paris: UNESCO.

Barth, F., 1973 a). "A General Perspective on Nomad–Sedentary Relations in the Middle East", in C. Nelson (ed.), *The Desert and the Sown. Nomads in the Wider Society*. Berkeley: Institute of International Studies, University of California.

Barth, F., 1973 b). "Descent and Marriage Reconsidered", in J. Goody (ed.), *The Character of Kinship*. Cambridge: Cambridge University Press.

Barth, F., 1982. "Problems in Conceptualizing Cultural Pluralism. With Illustration from Sohar, Oman", in D. Maybury-Lewis (ed.), *The Prospects for Plural Societies*. Washington: American Ethnological Society.

Barth, F., 1983. *Sohar: Culture and Society in an Omani Town*. Baltimore: Johns Hopkins University Press.

Barth, F., 1987. *Cosmologies in the Making*. Cambridge: Cambridge University Press.

Barth, F., 1989. "Are Values Real? The Enigma of Naturalism in the Anthropological Imputation of Values" (*mimeo*). University of Oslo.

Baumann, G., 1985. "Conversion and Continuity: Islamization among the Miri (Sudan)", *British Society for Middle Eastern Studies Bulletin*, 12 (2).

Baumann, G., 1987. *National Integration and Local Integrity. The Miri of the Nuba Mountains in the Sudan*. Oxford: Clarendon Press.

Bell, G.W., 1936. "Nuba Fertility Stones", *SNR*, XIX.

Bell, G.W., 1938. "Nuba Agricultural Methods and Beliefs", *SNR*, XXI.

Bell, G.W., 1983. *Shadows on the Sand. Memoirs of Sir Gawain Bell*. London: C. Hurst.

Bentley, G.C., 1987. "Ethnicity and Practice", *Comparative Studies in Society and History*, 29 (1).

Bentley, O and J.W. Crawfoot, 1924. "Nuba Pots in the Gordon College", *SNR*, VII.

Birks, J.S., 1978. *Across the Savannas to Mecca. The Overland Pilgrimage Route from West Africa*. London: C. Hurst.

Bjørkelo, A., 1976. *State and Society in Three Central Sudanic Kingdoms: Kanem-Bornu, Bigirmi and Wadai*. Unpublished M.A. thesis, University of Bergen.

Bjørkelo, A., 1983. *From King to Kashif. Shendi in the 19th century*. Doctoral Thesis, University of Bergen.

Bjørkelo, A., 1989. *Prelude to the Mahdiyya. Peasants and Traders in the Shendi Region, 1821–1885*. Cambridge: Cambridge University Press.

Born, M., 1965. *Bauern und Nomaden im Central Kordofan*. Marburg: Geografisches Institut der Universität Marburg.

Boserup, E., 1965. *The Conditions of Agricultural Growth. The Economics of Agrarian Change under Population Pressure*. London: George Allen & Unwin.

Brett, M., 1973. *Northern Africa: Islam and Modernization*. London: Franc Cass.

Brookfield, H., 1972. "Intensification and Disintensification in Pacific Agriculture. A Theoretical Approach", *Pacific Viewpoint*, Vol. 13.

Burnham, P., 1980 a). *Opportunity and Constraint in a Savanna Society. The Gbaya of Meiganga, Cameroon*. London: Academic Press.

Burnham, P., 1980 b). "Changing Agricultural and Pastoral Ecologies in the West African Savanna Region", in D.R. Harris (ed.), *Human Ecology in Savanna Environments*. London: Academic Press.

Carcereri, S., 1974. "In the Nuba Mountains, 1873", in E. Toniolo and R. Hill (eds.), *The Opening of the Nile Basin. Writings by Members of the Catholic Mission to Central Africa on the Geography and Ethnography of the Sudan. 1842–1881*. London: C. Hurst.

Carroll, L., 1977. " 'Sanscritization', 'Westernization' and 'Social Mobility': A

Reappraisal of the Relevance of Anthropological Concepts to the Social Historian in Modern India", *Journal of Anthropological Studies*, 33 (4).

Charsley, S.R., 1976. "The *Silika*: A Comparative Labour Organization", *Africa*, 46.

Chayanov, A.V., 1966. *The Theory of Peasant Economy*. D. Thorner, B. Kerblay, and R.E.F. Smith (eds.), Homewood, Illinois: American Economic Association.

Cohen, A., 1969. *Customs and Politics in Urban Africa. A study of Hausa Migrants in Yoruba towns*. London: Routledge & Kegan Paul.

Colson, E., 1958. *Marriage and Family among the Plateau Tonga*. Manchester: Manchester University Press.

Crawfoot, J.W., 1925. "Further Notes on Pottery (II. Lafofa Pottery)", *SNR*, VIII.

Cunnison, I., 1966. *Baggara Arabs*. Oxford: Clarendon Press.

Daly, M., 1980. *British Administration and the Northern Sudan, 1917–1924. The Governor-Generalship of Sir Lee Stack in the Sudan*. Leiden: Nederlands Historisch-archaeologisch Instituut.

Daly, M. (ed.), 1985. *Al Majdhubiyya and Al Mikashfiyaa: Two Sufi Tariqas in the Sudan*. Khartoum: Khartoum University Press.

Delmet, C., 1979. "Islamisation et Matrilinearite au Dar Fung (Soudan)", *L'Homme*, XIX (2).

Derman, W., 1973. *Serfs, Peasants and Socialists. A Former Serf Village in the Republic of Guinea*. Berkeiy: University of California Press.

Donham, D., 1979. *Production in a Malle Community, Southwestern Ethiopia, 1974–75*. Ph.D. Thesis, Stanford University.

Donham, D., 1980. "Beyond the Domestic Mode of Production", *Man*, 16.

Doornbos, P., 1984. "Trade in Two Border Towns: Beida and Foro Borang (Darfur Province)", in L. Manger (ed.), *Trade and Traders in the Sudan*. Bergen: Bergen Studies in Social Anthropology, No. 32.

Douglas, M., 1969. "Is Matriliny Doomed in Africa?", in M. Douglas and P.M. Kaberry (eds.), *Man in Africa*. London: Tavistock.

Duffield, M., 1981. *Maiurno: Capitalism and Rural Life in the Sudan*. London: Ithaca.

El Bushra, S., 1972. "The Development of Industry in Greater Khartoum, Sudan", *East African Geographical Review*, 19.

El-Dawi, Taj-el-Anbia Ali, 1972. "Social Characteristics of Big Merchants and Businessmen in El Obeid", in I. Cunnison and W. James (eds.), *Essays in Sudan Ethnography*. London: C. Hurst.

El-Hassan, Ali Moh., 1976. *An Introduction to the Sudanese Economy*. Khartoum: Khartoum University Press.

Elles, R., 1935. "The Kingdom of Tegale", *SNR*, vol. XVIII.

Elles, R., 1948. "The Kingdom of Tegali, 1921–1946", *SNR*, XXIX.

Ewald, J., 1982. *Leadership and Social Change on an Islamic Frontier: The Kingdom of Tegali, 1780–1900*. Ph.D. Thesis, University of Wisconsin-Madison.

Ewald, J., 1984. "Taqali", in R. Weeks (ed.), *Muslim People*, Vol. 2.

Ewald, J., 1985. "Experience and Speculation: History and Founding Stories in the Kingdom of Taqali, 1780–1935", *The International Journal of African Historical Studies*, 18 (2).

Ewald, J., 1988. "Speaking, Writing, and Authority: Explorations in and from the Kingdom of Taqali", *Comparative Studies in Society and History*, Vol. 30, (2).

Faris, J., 1968. "Some Aspects of Clanship and Descent Amongst the Nuba of Southeastern Kordofan", *SNR*, 49.

Faris, J., 1969 a). "Sibling Terminology and Cross-Sex Behaviour: Data from the Southeastern Nuba Mountains", *American Anthropologist*, 71.

Faris, J., 1969 b). "Some Cultural Considerations of Duolineal Descent Organization", *Ethnology*, 8 (3).

Faris, J., 1971. "Southeastern Nuba Age Organization", in W. James and I. Cunnison (eds.), *Sudan Ethnography. Essays in Honour of E.E. Evans-Pritchard.* London: C. Hurst.

Faris, J., 1972. *Nuba Personal Art.* London: Duckworth.

Faris, J., 1973. "Pax Britannica and the Sudan: S.F. Nadel", in T. Asad (ed.), *Anthropology and the Colonial Encounter.* London: Ithaca Press.

Faris, J., 1984. "Nuba", in R. Weeks (ed.), *Muslim People*, Vol. 2. London: Aldwyen Press.

Faris, J., 1989. *Southeast Nuba Social Relations.* Aachen: Alano Verlag.

Fisher, H. J., 1973. "Conversion Reconsidered: Some Historical Aspects of Religious Conversion in Black Africa", *Africa,* 43 (1).

Fisher, H.J., 1985. "The Juggernaut's Apologia: Conversion to Islam in Black Africa", *Africa,* 55 (2).

Fortes, M., 1949. "Time and Social Structure: an Ashanti Case Study", in M. Fortes (ed.), *Social Structure.* Oxford: Clarendon Press.

Geertz, C., 1963. *Agricultural Involution. The Process of Ecological Change in Indonesia.* Berkeley: University of California Press.

Geertz, C., 1968. *Islam Observed.* New Haven: Yale University Press.

Geertz, C., 1973. "Thick Description: Towards an Interpretive Theory of Culture", in C. Geertz, *The Interpretation of Culture.* New York: Basic Books Inc.

Geertz, C., 1983. *Local Knowledge.* New York: Basic Books Inc.

Gellner, E., 1978. "Scale and Nation", in F. Barth (ed.), *Scale and Social Organization.* Oslo: Norwegian University Press.

Glantz, M.H. (ed.), 1977. *Desertification. Environmental Degradation in and around Arid Land.* Boulder, Colorado: Westview Press.

Goodenough, W., 1955. "A Problem in Malayo-Polynesian Social Organization", *American Anthropologist*, 57.

Goody, J. (ed.), 1958. *The Developmental Cycle of Domestic Groups.* Cambridge: Cambridge University Press.

Goody, J. (ed.), 1968. *Literacy in Traditional Societies.* Cambridge: Cambridge University Press.

Goody, J., 1971. *Technology, Tradition and the State in Africa.* London: Oxford University Press.

Goody, J., 1986. *The Logic of Writing and the Organization of Society.* Cambridge: Cambridge University Press.

Gough, K., 1961. "The Modern Disintegration of Matrilineal Descent Groups", in D. Schneider and K. Gough (eds.), *Matrilineal Kinship.* Berkeley: University of California Press.

Grønhaug, R., (n.d.). "Transaction and Signification: An Analytical Distinction in the Study of Social Interaction" (*mimeo*), University of Bergen.

Grønhaug, R., 1974. *Micro-Macro Relations. Social Organizations in Antalya, Southern Turkey.* Bergen: Bergen Studies in Social Anthropology, No.7.

Grønhaug, R., 1978. "Scale as a Variable in Analysis: Fields in Social Organization in Herat, Northwestern Afghanistan", in F. Barth (ed.), *Scale and Social Organization.* Oslo: Norwegian University Press.

Grønhaug, R., 1984. "Sjansen til å overtale. Replikk-forskjeller og styrkeforhold i inter-etniske rettsaker", in H. Eidheim (ed.), *Retorikk og mytedannelse.* Oslo: Institute for Social Anthropology, University of Oslo.

Gulliver, P.H., 1971. *Neighbours and Networks. The Idiom of Kinship in Social Action among the Ndendeuli of Tanzania.* Berkeley: University of California Press.

Hargey, T., 1981. *The Suppression of Slavery in the Sudan 1898–1939.* Doctoral Thesis, University of Oxford.

Harir, S., 1981. *Old-Timers and New-Comers. Politics and Ethnicity in a Sudanese Community.* Bergen: Bergen Studies in Social Anthropology, No. 29.

Harir, S., 1986. *The Politics of "Numbers". Mediatory Leadership and the Political Process Among the Beri "Zaghawa" of the Sudan.* Doctoral Thesis, University of Bergen.

Harris, D., 1979. "Continuities and Change in Tropical Savanna Environments", *Current Anthropology*, Vol. 20, (2).

Hasan, Y. F.(ed.), 1971. *Sudan in Africa.* Khartoum: Khartoum University Press.

Hassoun, I., 1952. "Western Migrations and Settlement in the Gezira", *SNR*, XXXIII.

Hawkesworth, D., 1932. "The Nuba Proper of Southern Kordofan", *SNR*, XV.

Hem, H.E., 1980. *The Happy Ingessana and Development. Underproduction, Divison of Labour and Market Integration in the Ingessana Hills of the Sudan.* M.Sc. Thesis, University of Bergen.

Hill, P., 1977. *Population, Prosperity and Poverty. Rural Kano 1900 and 1970.* Cambridge: Cambridge University Press.

Hill, P., 1982. *Dry Grain Farming Families. Hausaland (Nigeria) and Karnataka (India) compared.* Cambridge: Cambridge University Press.

Hill, R., 1959. *Egypt in the Sudan, 1820–1881.* London: Greenwood.

Hoben, A., 1973. *Land Tenure Among the Amhara of Ethiopia. The Dynamics of Cognatic Descent.* Chicago: University of Chicago Press.

Holroyd, T., 1836. "Notes on a Journey to Kordofan in 1836–37", in *Geographical Society*, 9.

Holt, P.M., 1961. *A Modern History of the Sudan.* London: Weidenfeld and Nicolson.

Holt, P.M., 1970. *The Mahdist State in the Sudan.* Oxford: Clarendon Press.

Holy, L., 1986. *Strategies and Norms in a Changing Matrilineal Society. Descent, Succession and Inheritance among the Toka of Zambia.* Cambridge: Cambridge University Press.

Horton, R., 1971. "African Conversion", *Africa* 41 (2).

Horton, R., 1975. "On the Rationality of Conversion", *Africa* 45 (3 and 4).

Howell, J., (ed.), 1974. *Local Government and Politics in the Sudan.* Khartoum: Khartoum University Press.

Huddleston, H., 1947. "Foreword", in S.F. Nadel (ed.), *The Nuba.* London: Oxford University Press.

Hunting Technical Services Ltd., 1980. *South Kordofan Central Districts Indicative Development Plan.* Elstree: Hunting Technical Services.

Husmann, R., 1984. *Transkulturation bei den Nuba. Ethnologische Aspekte des kulturel-len Wandels im 19. und 20. Jahrhundert.* Göttingen: Edition Herodot.

Hutchinson, B., 1979. "Alcohol as a Contributing Factor in Social Disorganiza-tion: The South African Bantu in the Nineteenth Century", in M. Marshall (ed.), *Beliefs, Behaviours and Alcoholic Beverages.* Ann Arbor: University of Michigan Press.

Håland, G., 1969. "Economic Determinants in Ethnic Processes", in F. Barth (ed.), *Ethnic Groups and Boundaries.* Oslo: Norwegian University Press.

Håland, G., 1972. "Nomadism as an Economic Career Among the Sedentaries of the Sudan Savanna Belt", in I. Cunnison and W. James (eds.), *Essays in Sudan Ethnography.* London: C. Hurst.

Håland, G., 1977. "Pastoral Systems of Production. The Socio-Cultural Context and Some Economic and Ecological Implications", in P. O'Keefe and B. Wisner (eds.), *Land Use and Development.* London: International African Insti-tute and Environment Training Programme, UNEP–IDEP–SIDA.

Håland, G., 1978. "Ethnic Groups and Language Use in Darfur", in R. Thelwall (ed.), *Aspects of Language in the Sudan.* Ulster: New University of Ulster.

Håland, G. (ed.), 1980. *Problems of Savanna Development. The Sudan Case.* Bergen: Bergen Studies in Social Anthropology, No. 19.

Håland, G., 1990. "Beer, Blood and Mother's Milk. The Symbolic Context of Eco-nomic Behaviour in Fur", *Journal of Norwegian Anthropology*, 1. (in Norwegian).

Ibrahim, A.U.M., 1985. *The Dilemma of British Rule in the Nuba Mountains 1898–1947.* Khartoum: Khartoum University Press.

Ibrahim, F. and H. Ruppert, 1984. "Wandel der Sozioökonomischen Struktur in den Nuba-Bergen (S-Kordofan) vor dem Hintergrund Intensiver Wan-derungsprozesse in die Konurbation Khartoum", *Paideuma* 30.

Ibrahim, F. and H. Ruppert, (eds.), 1988. *Rural-Urban Migration and Identity Change. Case Studies from the Sudan.* Bayreuth: Bayreuter Geowissenschaft-lische Arbeiten, Vol. 11.

ILO/UNDP Employment Mission, 1976. *Growth, Employment and Equity. A Com-prehensive Strategy for the Sudan.* Geneva: ILO.

Jahnke, H., 1980. *Livestock Production Systems and Livestock Development in Tropical Africa.* Kiel: Kieler Wissenschaftsverlag.

Jalil, Musa Adam A., 1984. "From Native Courts to People's Local Courts: the Politics of Judicial Administration in Sudan", Seminar Paper, 47. *Development Studies and Research Center*, University of Khartoum.

James, W., 1971. "Social Assimilation and Changing Identity in the Southern Funj", in Fadl Hasan (ed.), *Sudan in Africa.* Khartoum: Khartoum University Press.

James, W., 1972. "The Politics of Rain Control Among the Uduk", in I. Cunnison and W. James (eds.), *Essays in Sudan Ethnography.* Essays in honour of Sir E. Evans-Pritchard. London: C. Hurst.

James, W., 1977. "The Funj Mystique: Approaches to a Problem of Sudanese History", in R.K. Jain (ed.), *Text and Context: The Social Anthropology of Tradition.* Philadelphia, Pa.: Institute of the Study of Human Issues.

James, W., 1979. *"Kwanim Pa". The Making of the Uduk People.* Oxford: Clarendon Press.

Jedrej, M., 1974. "Cultural Borrowing and Social Assimilation in the Southern Funj: A Note on the Persistence of Ingessana Culture", *SNR*, 55.

Keesing, R., 1982. *Kwaio Religion*. New York: Columbia University Press.

Kenrick, J.W., 1945. "A Nuba Age-Grade Initiation Ceremony. The Sibrs of the Tail and of the Shield", *SNR*, XXVI.

Kerzani, I., 1983. "A Proposed Strategy for the Transformation of the Pre-Capitalist Part of the Sudanese Society" (*mimeo*). Khartoum: Development Studies and Economic Research Center.

Kottak, C.P., 1980. *The Past in the Present. History, Ecology and Cultural Variation in Highland Madagascar*. Ann Arbor: University of Michigan Press.

Levtzion, N., 1979. "Towards a Comparative Study of Islamization", in N. Levtzion (ed.), *Conversion to Islam*. New York: Holms & Meier.

Lewis, I. (ed.), 1963. "Introduction", in *Islam in Tropical Africa*. London: International African Institute.

Lewis, I. (ed.), 1983. "Syncretism and Survival in African Islam", in *Aspetti Dell'Islam "Marginale"*, Roma: Accademia Nazionale Dei Lincei.

Ludwig, H-D., 1968. "Permanent Farming on Ukara. The Impact of Land Shortage on Husbandry Practices", in H. Ruthenberg (ed.), *Smallholder Farming and Smallholder Development in Tanzania*. München: Weltforum Verlag.

MacDiarmid, D.N., 1927. "Notes on Nuba Customs and Languages", *SNR*, X.

MacDiarmid, P.A. & D.N., 1931. "The Languages of the Nuba Mountains", *SNR*, XIV.

MacGaffey, W., 1961. "The History of Negro Migrations in the Northern Sudan", *Southwestern Journal of Anthropology*, 17 (2).

MacMichael, H., 1967. *The Tribes of Northern and Central Kordofan*. London: Frank Cass.

Mahmoud. A. I., 1980. *The History of the Isma'iliyya Tariqa in the Sudan: 1792–1914*. Doctoral Thesis, University of London.

Manger, L.O., 1978. "Some Remarks on the Use of Labour in Kheiran, The Sudan", in E. Eriksen, et al., *Aspects of Agro-Pastoral Adaptations in East Africa*. Bergen: Bergen Studies in Social Anthropology, No. 13.

Manger, L., 1979. "Public Schemes and Local Participation: Some Remarks on the Present Situation in the Southern Nuba Mountains Area of the Sudan". Paper to the Conference: Planning, Agricultural Development and Popular Participation. *Development Studies and Research Center*, University of Khartoum.

Manger, L., 1980. "Cultivation Systems and the Struggle for Household Viability under Conditions of Desert Encroachment", in G. Håland (ed.), *Problems of Savanna Development*. Bergen, Bergen Studies in Social Anthropology. No. 19.

Manger, L., 1981. *The Sand Swallows Our Land. Over-Exploitation of Productive Resources and the Problem of Household Viability in the Kheiran—a Sudanese Oasis*. Bergen: Bergen Studies in Social Anthropology, No. 24.

Manger, L., (ed.), 1984. *Trade and Traders in the Sudan*. Bergen: Bergen Studies in Social Anthropology, No. 32.

Manger, L., 1984. "Traders and Farmers in the Nuba Mountains: Jellaba Family Firms in the Liri Area", in L. Manger (ed.), *Trade and Traders in the Sudan*. Bergen: Bergen Studies in Social Anthropology, No. 32.

Manger, L., (ed.), 1987. *Communal Labour in the Sudan*. Bergen: Bergen Studies in Social Anthropology, No. 41.

Manger, L., 1987 a). "Communal Labour among the Lafofa: Vehicle of Economic and Social Change", in L. Manger (ed.), *Communal Labour in the Sudan*. Bergen: Bergen Studies in Social Anthropology, No. 41.

Manger, L., 1987 b). "Agricultural Intensification and Resource Maintenance. Some Cases from Western Sudan", in Mohamed A.R. Salih (ed.), *Agrarian Change in the Central Rainlands: Sudan*. Uppsala: Scandinavian Institute of African Studies.

Manger, L., 1988. "Traders, Farmers and Pastoralists. Economic Adaptations and Environmental Problems in the Southern Nuba Mountains of the Sudan", in D. Anderson & D. Johnson (eds.), *The Ecology of Survival: Case Studies from Northeast African History*. London: Lester Crook Academic Publ.

Manger, L., 1990. "Agro-Pastoral Production Systems and the Problem of Resource Management", in M. Bovin and L. Manger (eds.), *Adaptive Strategies in African Arid Lands*. Uppsala: Scandinavian Institute of African Studies.

Manger, L., 1991. "From Slave to Citizen. Processes of Cultural Change among the Lafofa Nuba of Central Sudan", in R. Grønhaug, G. Henriksen and G. Håland (eds.), *The Ecology of Choice and Symbol. Festschrift for Fredrik Barth*. Bergen: Alma Mater.

Marriott, M., 1955. "Little Communities in an Indigeneous Civilization", in M. Marriott (ed.), *Village India. Studies in the Little Community*. Chicago: University of Chicago Press.

Martini, G., 1974. "People and Government in the Nuba Mountains", in E. Toniolo and R. Hill (eds.), *The Opening of the Nile Basin. Writings by Members of the Catholic Mission to Central Africa on the Geography and Ethnography of the Sudan 1842–1881*. London: C. Hurst.

McCown, R.L., G. Håland and C. de Haan, 1979. "The Interaction Between Cultivation and Livestock Production in Semi-Arid Africa", in A.E. Hall, G.H. Cannell and H.W. Lawton (eds.), *Agriculture in Semi-Arid Environments*. Berlin: Springer Verlag.

McLoughlin, P., 1962. "Economic Development and the Heritage of Slavery in the Sudan Republic", *Africa*, 32.

McLoughlin, P. (ed.), 1970. "Introduction", in *African Food Production Systems. Cases and Theory*. Baltimore: Johns Hopkins Press.

Mercer, P., 1971. "Shilluk Trade and Politics from the Mid-Seventeenth Century to 1861", *Journal of African History*, XII, 3.

Mines, M., 1975. "Islamization and Muslim Ethnicity in South India", *Man*, 10.

Mitchell, C., 1956. *The Yao Village*. Manchester: Manchester University Press.

Nadel, S., 1947. *The Nuba, An Anthropological Study of the Hill Tribes of Kordofan*. Oxford: Oxford University Press.

Nadel, S., 1950. "Dual Descent in the Nuba Hills", in D. Forde and A.E. Radcliffe-Brown (eds.), *African Systems of Kinship and Marriage*. London: Oxford University Press.

Nadel, S., 1952. "Witchcraft in Four African Societies: an Essay in Comparison", *American Anthropologist*, 54.

Nadel, S., 1955. "Two Nuba religions: an Essay in Comparison", *American Anthropologist*, 57.

Nasr, Ahmed A. Rahim, 1971. "British Policy Towards Islam in the Nuba Mountains, 1920–1940", *Sudan Notes and Records (SNR)* LII.

Netting, R., 1964. "Beer as a Locus of Value among the West African Kofyar", *American Anthropologist*, 66.

Netting, R., 1965. "Household Organization and Intensive Agriculture: the Kofyar Case", *Africa*, 35.

Netting, R., 1968. *Hill Farmers of Nigeria. Cultural Ecology of the Kofyar of the Jos Plateau*. Seattle: University of Washington Press.

Netting, R., 1974. "Agrarian Ecology", *Annual Review of Anthropology*, Vol. 3.

Nypan, A., 1971. *Sociological Aspects of Agricultural Development. A Case Study from Two Areas in Uganda*. Section for Development Studies, Dept. of Sociology, University of Oslo. Report No. 5.

O'Brien, J., 1977. *How "Traditional" is Traditional Agriculture?* Khartoum: Economic and Social Research Council, Bulletin 62.

O'Fahey, R.S., 1971. "Religion and Trade in the Keira Sultanate of Darfur", in Y. Fadl Hasan (ed.), *Sudan in Africa*. Khartoum: Khartoum University Press.

O'Fahey, R.S., 1980. *State and Society in Darfur*. London: C. Hurst.

O'Fahey, R.S., 1982. "Fur and Fartit: The History of a Frontier", in J. Mack and P. Robertshaw (eds.), *Culture History in the Southern Sudan*. Nairobi: Memoir of the British Institute of Eastern Africa, No. 8.

O'Fahey, R.S., 1985. "Slavery and Society in Darfur", in J.R. Willis (ed.), *Slaves and Society in Muslim Africa*. (in Vol.2). London: Frank Cass.

O'Fahey, R.S. and J. Spaulding, 1972. "Hashim and the Mussabba'at", *Bulletin for the School of Oriental and African Studies*, XXXV/2.

O'Fahey, R.S. and J. Spaulding, 1974 *Kingdoms of the Sudan*. London: Methuen & Co.

O'Fahey, R.S. and A.S. Karrar, 1987. "The Enigmatic Imam: The Influence of Ahmad Ibn Idris", *International Journal of Middle Eastern Studies*, 19.

O'Loughlin, M.B., 1973. *Mbum Beer Parties*. Ph.D. Thesis, Yale University.

Orans, M., 1965. *The Santal. A Tribe in Search of a Great Tradition*. Detroit: Wayne State University Press.

Osman, Abdel Hamid M., 1986. *The Hawazma Baggara. Some Issues and Problems in Pastoral Adaptations*. M.A. Thesis. University of Bergen.

Peney, A., 1883. "L'Ethnographie du Soudan Egyptien: Troisième Mémoire: Daher et Tagala", *Revue d'Ethnographie*, Vol. II.

Petherick, J., 1861. *Egypt, the Soudan and Central Africa*. Edinburgh: William Blackwood.

Poewe, K., 1978 a). "Matriliny in the Throes of Change. Kinship, Descent and Marriage in Luapula, Zambia", *Africa*, 48 (3 and 4).

Poewe, K., 1978 b). "Matriliny and Capitalism: The Development of Incipient Classes in Luapula, Zambia", *Dialectical Anthropology*, 3.

Poewe, K., 1978 c). "Religion, Matriliny and Change: Jehovah's Witnesses and Seventh-Day Adventists in Luapula, Zambia", *American Ethnologist* 5.

Poewe, K., 1980. "Matrilineal Ideology: The Economic Activities of Women in Luapula, Zambia", in L.S. Cordelol and S.S. Beckerman (eds.), *The Versatility of Kinship*. New York: Academic Press.

Poewe, K. and P.R. Lovell, 1980. "Marriage, Descent and Kinship. On the Differential Primacy of Institutions in Luapula (Zambia) and Longana (New Hebridies)", *Africa*, 50 (1).

Redfield, R., 1960. *The Little Community*. Chicago: Chicago University Press.

Richards, A., 1939. *Land, Labour and Diet in Northern Rhodesia*. London: Oxford University Press.

Richards, A., 1950. "Some Types of Family Structures Amongst the Central Bantu", in D. Forde and A.E. Radcliffe-Brown (eds.), *African Systems of Kinship and Marriage*. London: Oxford University Press.

Richards, A., 1971. "Matrilineal Systems", in J. Goody (ed.), *Kinship: Selected Read-ings*. Harmondsworth: Penguin.

Rigby, P., 1981. "Pastors and Pastoralists: The Differential Penetration of Chris-tianity among East African Cattle Herders", *Comparative Studies in Society and History*, 23 (1).

Roden, D., 1972. "Down Migration in the Moro Hills of Southern Kordofan", *SNR*, LIII.

Rottenburg, R., 1988. *Die Lemwareng-Nuba. Ein Beispiel kultureller Akkreszenz im heutigen Nil-Sudan*. Abridged version of Doctoral Thesis, Freie Universität, Berlin.

Ruppel, E., 1829. *Reisen in Nubien, Kordofan und dem petraeischen Arabien*. Chapters 16–20. Frankfurt.

Rusegger, J., 1844. *Reise in Egypten, Nubien und Ost-Sudan*. Part II, p. 344–361. Stuttgart.

Ruthenberg, H., 1976. *Farming Systems in the Tropics*. Oxford: Clarendon Press.

Sagar, J.W., 1922. "Notes on the History, Religion and Customs of the Nuba", *SNR*, V.

Salih, Mohamed A.R., 1983. *Development and Social Change among the Moro of the Nuba Mountains*. Doctoral Thesis, University of Manchester.

Sahlins, M., 1965. "On the Ideology and Composition of Descent Groups", *Man* 65.

Salamone, F., 1975. "Becoming Hausa: Ethnic Identity Change and Its Implica-tions for the Study of Ethnic Pluralism and Stratification", *Africa*, 45, (5).

Sanderson, L., 1963. "Educational Development and Administrative Control in the Nuba Mountains Region of the Sudan", *Journal of African History*, IV, 2.

Sangree, W.H., 1962. "The Social Function of Beer Drinking in Bantu Tiriki", in Pittman, D.J. & C.R. Snyder (eds.), *Society, Culture and Drinking Patterns*. New York: Wiley.

Scheffler, H., 1966. "Ancestor Worship in Anthropology: Or—Observations on Descent and Descent Groups", *Current Anthropology*, 7 (5).

Schneider, D., 1961. "The Distinctive Features of Matrilineal Descent Groups", in D. Schneider and C. Gough (eds.), *Matrilineal Kinship*. Berkeley: University of California Press.

Schultz, E., 1984. "From Pagan to Pullo: Ethnic Identity Change in Northern Cameroon", *Africa*, 54 (1).

Schwartz, T., 1978. "The Size and Shape of a Culture", in F. Barth (ed.), *Scale and Social Organization*. Oslo: Norwegian University Press.

Seligman, C.G., 1914. "A Note on the Magico-Religious Aspect of Iron Working in Southern Kordofan", *Annals of Archaeology and Anthropology*, 6.

Seligman, C.G., 1959. "Nuba", in J. Hastings (ed.), *Encyclopedia of Religion and Ethics*, Vol. 9. New York, C. Scribner's Sons.

Seligman, C.G. and B.Z., 1932. "The Nuba", in C.G. and B.Z. Seligman: *Pagan Tribes of the Nilotic Sudan*. London: Routledge & Kegan Paul.

Shazeli, S., 1980. *Beyond Underdevelopment. Structural Constraints on the Development of Productive Forces among the Jok Gor in the Sudan*. Bergen: Bergen Studies in Social Anthropology, No. 22.

Skinner, E., 1958. "Christianity and Islam among the Mossi", *American An-thropologist*, LX.

Simmons, W., 1979. "Islamic Conversion and Social Change in a Senegalese Village", *Ethnology*, 18.

Spaulding, J., 1980. "Towards a Demystification of the Funj: Some Perspectives on Society in Southern Sinnar, 1685–1900", *Northeast African Studies*, 2 (1).

Spaulding, J., 1982. "Slavery, Land Tenure and Social Class in the Northern Turkish Sudan", *The International Journal of African Historical Studies*, 15 (1).

Spaulding, J., 1985. *The Heroic Age in Sinnar*. East Lansing: African Studies Center, Michigan State University.

Srinivas, M.N., 1966. *Social Change in Modern India*. Berkeley: University of California Press.

Stenning, D., 1958. "Household Viability among the Pastoral Fulani", in J. Goody, (ed.), *The Development Cycle of Domestic Groups*. Cambridge: Cambridge University Press.

Stenning, D., 1959. *Savanna Nomads*. London: Oxford University Press.

Stevenson, R., 1956. "A Survey of the Phonetics and Grammatical Structure of the Nuba Mountain Languages. With Particular Reference to Otoro, Katcha and Nyimang", *Afrika und Übersee*. Band XL, Heft 4.

Stevenson, R., 1961. "The Doctrine of God in the Nuba Mountains", in E.W. Smith (ed.), *African Ideas of God*. (Second edition revised and edited by E.G. Parrinder). London: Edinburgh House Press.

Stevenson, R., 1962. "Linguistic Research in the Nuba Mountains I", *SNR*, XLIII.

Stevenson, R., 1964. "Linguistic Research in the Nuba Mountains II", *SNR*, XLV.

Stevenson, R., 1966. "Some Aspects of the Spread of Islam in the Nuba Mountains", in I. Lewis (ed.), *Islam in Tropical Africa*. London: International African Institute.

Stevenson, R., 1984. *The Nuba People of Kordofan Province. An Ethnographic Survey*. Khartoum: Khartoum University Press.

Storås, F., 1976. *The Acholi Tribe* (mimeo). University of Bergen.

Swift, J., 1977. "Desertification and Man in the Sahel", in P. O'Keefe and B. Wisner (eds.), *Landuse and Development*. London: International African Institute, Environmental Training Programme, UNEP–IDEP–SIDA.

Szolc, P., 1977. "Die Konsequenzen der Islamisierung in Kordofan", *Africana Marburgensia*, 10.

Sørbø, G., 1977. "Nomads on the Scheme—A Study of Irrigation Agriculture and Pastoralism in Eastern Sudan", in P. O'Keefe and B. Wisner (eds.), *Landuse and Development*. London: International African Institute, Environmental Training Programme, UNEP–IDEP–SIDA.

Sørbø, G., 1982. "Maintenance and Change of Production Systems" (*mimeo*). University of Bergen.

Sørbø, G., 1985. *Tenants and Nomads in Eastern Sudan. A Study of Economic Adaptations in the New Halfa Scheme*. Uppsala: Scandinavian Institute of African Studies.

Tanzenmüller, K., 1885. "Das Gebiet der Shilluk und Bakara, Dar Nubah, Taklah und Kordofan", *Deutsche Rundschau für Geographie und Statistik*, VII.

Timberlake, L., 1985. *Africa in Crisis*. London: Earthscan.

Tothill, J. (ed.), 1948. *Agriculture in the Sudan*. London: Oxford University Press.

Trimingham, J.S., 1949. *Islam in the Sudan*. London: Frank Cass & Co.

Tuden, A. and L. Plotnicov, 1970. "Introduction", in A. Tuden and L. Plotnicov (eds.), *Social Stratification in Africa*. New York: Free Press.

Turner, V., 1957. *Schism and Continuity in an African Society*. Manchester: Manchester University Press.

Turner, V., 1967. *The Forest of Symbols: Aspects of Ndembu Ritual*. New York: Ithaca Press.

Vicars-Miles, A.L.W., 1930. *The Kawahla of Kalogi*. Government Report in Talodi Rural Council. Unclassified.

Vicars-Miles, A.L.W., 1934. "The Nuba Mountains—their Past and Future", in *Sudan Archive*, Durham, 631/10.

Vincze, L., 1980. "Peasant Animal Husbandry: A Dialectical Model of Techno-Environmental Integration in Agro-Pastoral Societies", *Ethnology* IXIX, 4.

Warburg, G., 1971. *The Sudan Under Wingate*. London: Frank Cass.

Watson, R.M., 1976. *Sudan National Livestock Census and Resource Inventory*. Volumes 03, 04, 05, 24. Khartoum: Sudan Veterinary Research Administration.

Wilmington, M., 1955. "Aspects of Moneylending in Northern Sudan", *The Middle East Journal*, 9.

Wilson, M., 1977. *For Men and Elders. Change in the Relations of Generations and of Men and Women among the Nyakyusa-Ngonde People 1875–1971*. New York: Africana Publishing Company.

Index